THE
CONCORDE
STORY

THE
CONCORDE
STORY

Christopher Orlebar

HAMLYN

Endpapers

These charts show Concorde's west and east bound Atlantic tracks, 'SM' and 'SN' respectively; 'SO' is a reserve track. The acceleration and deceleration points, labelled 'ACCEL' and 'DECEL', are the points respectively where Concorde either commences acceleration from Mach 0.95, or deceleration from Mach 2. However, the deceleration point is varied a few miles either side of the position shown depending on the conditons – aircraft altitude and forecast wind – prevalent on the day.

There are a variety of routes into the United States, however the route to New York via Linnd and Sates is the one described in the chapter, The Flight – Deceleration. Concorde must cross the boundary of the 'warning area' (W105 BDY) above 52,000 ft when that area is 'active' with military training or test flights.

The front inset shows a plan view of the runways at Heathrow with the designations as they were when Concorde entered service in 1976: 10L, 10R, 28L and 28R. The ever-reducing magnetic variation in Britain has brought their tracks closer to 090°M and, in the opposite direction, 270°M, than to the 100°M and 280°M they used to approximate to. (°M is the measure of the direction with respect to magnetic north.) Therefore, since July 1987, they have been called: 09L, 09R, 27L, and 27R.

The back inset shows the approach path to runway 4R (the right-hand of the two northeast facing runways) at Kennedy – the runway onto which the landing was made in the chapter, The Flight – Deceleration.

Half title page

One of the few photographs taken of Concorde actually in supersonic flight. This picture was taken from a Panavia Tornado.

'Oh God, who art the author of peace, and lover of concord. . . '
From the second Collect, for Peace in the Book of Common Prayer

To my wife Nicola and our children Edward and Caroline. CO

First published 1986 by Temple Press
an imprint of The Hamlyn Publishing Group Limited,
Michelin House, 81 Fulham Road,
London SW3 6RB

© Copyright The Hamlyn Publishing Group Limited
1986, 1990 and 1994

Eighth impression 1994

ISBN 0 600 58515 8

Edited by Tony Holmes

Produced by Mandarin Offset
Printed and bound in Hong Kong

Cover and back cover photographs by Mark Wagner

Contents

Acknowledgements

'The Concorde Story' was originally published in 1986 to celebrate Concorde's first ten years in service. This new edition reflects on where Concorde has taken civil supersonic flight and, in the light of new technology, what might follow Concorde. Also included is a chapter about the selection and training of a Concorde pilot.

I would like to acknowledge the encouragement that I received from British Airways, without whose co-operation writing this book, whilst being a practising pilot, would have been a daunting prospect. In particular I must thank Brian Walpole who suggested that I should be its author, Mike Ramsden, former Editor in Chief of *Flight International*, who reinforced Brian's confidence. My children, Edward and Caroline, need special mention for having put up with my being closeted for hours in my study during what should have been time off with them. Thanks to my wife Nicola and her sister Angela for deciphering and typing the original hand-written pages, I have since learnt to use a word processor. Commendation is due to my neighbours, Peter Leggett, Fellow of the Royal Aeronautical Society and former Vice-Chancellor of Surrey University, and his wife Enid, who gave me immense assistance in suggesting improvements in the script. Charles Burnet, formerly of British Aerospace Weybridge and an expert in aircraft development cost analysis (he noted that costs rise with increasing length to span ratio), gave invaluable help in checking the historical and technical facts of the book as well as its style. His book *Three Centuries to Concorde* sparked my enthusiasm for the history of supersonic flight.

The greatest acknowledgement must go to the people who designed, built, maintain and fly Concorde, and to the passengers, who by continuing to use Concorde, have ensured its ultimate success. Without them this extraordinary aircraft would have come to naught and there would have been no story. Furthermore, this success has spawned serious interest in the eventual building of a successor to Concorde.

Christopher Orlebar
Oxshott, May 1994

The author with Sir Frank Whittle on the flight deck of Concorde during the filming of 'Jet Trail', a documentary about the effect of jet propulsion on civil transport. May 1984

Foreword

by Captain Brian Walpole

Concorde is an outstanding aeroplane, it is a technical miracle, and more. For the men who designed and constructed it, the crews who tested it, for those in British Airways involved in its operation – flying it, maintaining it, marketing it – and for its passengers, Concorde is a way of life.

The story of Concorde is a story of survival. In its long history, it has been vulnerable in four main areas. Technically, environmentally, politically and economically. Many times it has stood close to extinction. But it survived, thanks to the dedication, faith and belief of those who controlled its destiny at the various critical phases of its life.

Its design, construction and maintenance teams have overcome many and varied problems, and now, ten years into airline service, we have a safe, proven, reliable and totally unparalleled piece of aviation technology flying the world's air routes. It is confidently predicted that it will fly into the 21st century; many indeed suggest that this is where its technology came from in the first place.

Politically, it has come through the vicissitudes of national and international politics until, today, it stands free from political influence. Environmentally, its operation has been skilfully tailored to meet acceptance almost worldwide. Economically, it represents a major contribution to British Airways' profitability and a unique asset of unquantifiable value as the airline's flagship.

The faith of those who believed that Concorde represented a technical achievement of enormous magnitude which should not be allowed to perish, has been fully vindicated. All who have contributed to this magnificent aircraft and the way of life it represents are today justifiably proud of 'the beautiful bird – Concorde'.

Captain Brian Walpole, O.B.E., General Manager, Concorde Division of British Airways 1982–1988

H.M. The Queen Mother's birthday present from British Airways was a trip in Concorde on 6 August 1985. Seen here with Captain Walpole (centre) and Senior Engineer Officer, Peter Phillips (right)

Preface

This book is about the conquest of flight at speeds faster than sound. It covers the synthesis of the host of disciplines which were brought together to build and operate the most superlative form of transport yet built by man – Concorde. Yet Concorde exists in the ordinary physical world. There was no divine intervention which altered the laws of nature to favour Concorde. Its success has been achieved by the devotion of countless people who have been inspired by the concept. It ranks with the architectural marvels of the world – the Pyramids, the Gothic Cathedrals and the Taj Mahal.

This book was written to commemorate Concorde's first ten years in commercial service – from 21 January 1976 to 21 January 1986.

What follows is a brief description of some of the technical terms and concepts that the more inquisitive reader may find useful. In some instances these are expanded in the chapters that follow.

*1838–1916.

The airspeed indicator on Concorde showing just over 500 knots, whilst the Machmeter indicates just less than Mach 2 corresponding to a true airspeed of 1,150 knots. The apparent discrepancy is due to the low density of the air found at 53,000 ft causing the aircraft to 'feel' only 500 knots. See the 'Flight envelope' on page 122

Ernst Mach*, an Austrian physicist, observed that airflows obeyed different laws as they approached the speed of sound. In recognition of his work, the term 'Mach number' was named after him. The Mach number of a moving body is the ratio of its speed to that of the speed of sound in the fluid in which it is travelling. The fluid in which aircraft travel is, of course, the air in the atmosphere. When an aircraft's speed is the same as the speed of sound it is said to have a Mach number of one – Mach 1.

Ernst Mach was a positivist who argued strongly against the notion that matter was made up of atoms. The explanation of why the airflow obeyed different laws, as the speed of sound is approached, is much easier to explain on the assumption that atoms and molecules exist. It is therefore curious that Mach did not agree with what has now become the accepted truth.

Air is a gas which is made up of molecules moving randomly at high speed. Their speed varies with temperature. They move more quickly when it is hot than when it is cold. The speed of sound in air is the speed at which vibrations or changes of pressure are transmitted through the air. As this speed is a function of the speed the molecules move,

sound travels quicker in hot air than in cold.

At 15°C (59°F), the average temperature found at sea level, the speed of sound is about 760 mph (660 knots). Between 50,000 ft and 60,000 ft, where the temperature averages minus 57°C (−71°F), it is 660 mph (573 knots). It varies in fact with the square root of absolute temperature (absolute zero is minus 273°C (−459.4°F) thus the freezing point of water is 273° Kelvin and its boiling point 373°K, etc).

An aircraft in flight can be travelling subsonically, i.e. below the speed of sound, or supersonically, i.e. above the speed of sound. The airflow, as Mach observed, is governed by two quite different laws depending on whether the aircraft is flying at subsonic or supersonic speeds. There is, however, a third definition of speed, and that is 'transonic'. In reality 'transonic' refers to a range of speeds typically from Mach 0.75 to Mach 1.3. It is called 'transonic' because both supersonic and subsonic (governed by their respective laws) are present simultaneously.

At first sight it is not obvious why a supersonic airflow can be present when an aircraft is flying subsonically. The reason is that an aircraft in flight separates the air. The airflow over the more bulbous parts of the aircraft (over a protruding cockpit or over the top of the wings) has to travel further than the air underneath the aircraft. Thus the air travelling the further distance over the aircraft has to travel more quickly. To be consistent with the law of energy conservation, as the 'moving' energy of the air increases, its pressure energy must reduce. Low pressure on the top surface of a wing sucks it upwards, or gives it 'lift'. When the speed of an aircraft exceeds about Mach 0.75 the faster moving air over the wings reaches Mach 1. Therefore supersonic airflow is found on an aircraft flying subsonically.

When the aircraft flies faster than Mach 1 some of the air, depending on the shape of the aircraft, is pulled along by the aircraft, so that part flows subsonically over the surface. Usually by the time the aircraft has reached about Mach 1.3 all the airflow over it is supersonic. Flight at transonic speeds was to prove more difficult than flight at supersonic speeds.

As an aircraft flies it experiences resistance from the air. This is known as 'drag'. The amount of lift compared to drag that an aircraft experiences at a given speed is a measure of its aerodynamic efficiency. This is known as the lift to drag ratio,

commonly written as L/D. Drag is caused by the shape of the aircraft (form drag), by the surface of the aircraft (skin friction drag) and by the work the wings have to do to give lift (induced drag). The first two increase with speed, while induced drag decreases with speed.

At speeds below about 300 knots (1 knot = 1.15 mph), the airflow over an aircraft behaves like an incompressible fluid (like water). Above 300 knots the molecules of air, having had less 'warning' of the impending disturbance, become compressed. The 'warning' travels at the speed of sound. As the aircraft travels closer to Mach 1 the molecules have progressively less time in which to redistribute themselves before the passage of the aircraft. Now they build up and make, at Mach 1, a distinct 'compression wave' or 'shock wave'. This wave, analogous to a bow wave of a boat, increases the drag. Hence the notion that there was some kind of barrier at Mach 1, although projectiles like bullets had exceeded the speed of sound for over two hundred years. At the rear of an aircraft flying above Mach 1 is another compression wave where the air reverts to its original condition, having steadily reduced to a lower pressure during the passage of the aircraft. These two shock waves can usually be heard on the ground as a double boom.

At first sight it is difficult to visualise that

The shock waves formed in the air around a supersonic aircraft are analogous to the waves formed by a moving boat. Here water is flowing over a thin silhouette of Concorde to demonstrate the analogy. Although these waves are formed in just two dimensions, the shock waves on an aircraft are in three dimensions, forming a cone at the nose the air ahead of an object moving at subsonic speed starts to redistribute itself before the arrival of the object. Observation of light airborne objects, like snowflakes or thistle seeds, becoming wafted over the windscreen of a moving car demonstrates the effect. Heavier objects like grit and raindrops do not deflect. Should the car accelerate towards Mach 1, the deflection of even the light objects would not happen. Their first 'knowledge' of the car would be the car itself.

Once the sound barrier had been 'broken' another barrier appeared – the heat barrier. The faster an aircraft flies the more it is heated by the air which surrounds it. This is not an effect which is suddenly manifest, as it is present at all speeds, but does not become significant until the aircraft is travelling supersonically. It is caused by the compression of the air as it is accelerated during the passage of the aircraft. When any gas is compressed its temperature rises, as is readily observed when pumping up a

Wind tunnel models of Concorde were used to check its viability throughout the speed range. Here flight at slow speeds, requiring high angles of attack, is about to be investigated

bicycle tyre. The end of the pump becomes very hot due to the compression of the air within it. On an aircraft this effect is known as kinetic heating.

The temperature rise in degrees centigrade can be calculated approximately by squaring the true airspeed in mph of the aircraft and dividing this by 100. At Mach 2, about 1,320 mph, the rise is 174°C (345°F); at Mach 3 it is 392°C (737°F). These quantities are for the point experiencing the greatest temperature rise, usually the tip of the

aircraft's nose, where the air is accelerated to the speed of the aircraft. To this figure must be added the static air temperature. Above 37,000 ft this averages minus 57°C (−71°F), varying from place to place over the globe. At Mach 2 the final top temperature is thus 117°C (243°F) and at Mach 3 it is 335°C (635°F). Kinetic heating has an immense bearing on the choice of cruising speed for a supersonic transport aircraft (SST) and the materials from which it will be built. Aluminium alloys can easily cope with temperatures up to about 130°C (266°F); higher than that, more expensive titanium alloys must be used.

To monitor the temperature experienced by the nose of fast moving aircraft there is a gauge in the cockpit. It simply reads degrees centigrade. There are other instruments like the altimeter and compass which say, with a fair degree of accuracy, how high the aircraft is and in which direction it is pointing. There is one instrument, however, which to the untutored eye appears as if it is constantly telling a frightful lie (unless it is observed at sea level) and that is the airspeed indicator.

At sea level the speed shown on the airspeed indicator corresponds quite closely to the True Airspeed (TAS). But as the aircraft climbs into the thinner air the indicator registers an airspeed which is less than true. At Mach 2 and 55,000 ft the true airspeed would be 1,150 knots, but because of the low density of the air, the indicated airspeed is only 500 knots.

Aircraft are flown with special reference to indicated airspeed since this is a measure of what the aircraft feels. Knowledge of what the aircraft 'feels' tells the pilots how the aircraft can perform; how close it is, for instance, to losing the ability to give lift (stalling). Or, in the case of Concorde, how much extra thrust will be required to overcome the high induced drag when flying at landing speeds.

Indicated airspeed also shows the pilot how great an angle of attack the aircraft is experiencing. The angle of attack is the angle between the aircraft and the flow of air. As the speed falls so this angle increases, thus lift is maintained. If constant altitude is to be maintained during deceleration, the aircraft must be pitched up to compensate for the increased angle of attack. When descending to land, Concorde has quite a high pitch attitude (11°). This is because of the high angle of attack (14°) associated with low indicated airspeed.

The Background

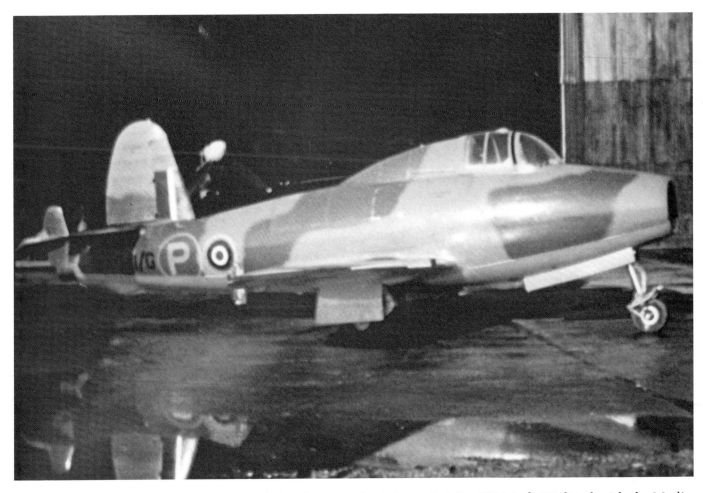

The E28/39 or Gloster-Whittle. Britain's first jet propelled aircraft, which first flew 14 May 1941. Its engine gave a modest 850 lb of thrust. The engine planned for the US SST was to have given close on 70,000 lb of thrust

'Pull steadily, watch the altimeter, don't flap and don't expect anything much to happen until below 15,000 to 20,000 ft . . .' This advice was contained in a document written by George Bulman, Chief Test Pilot of Hawker Aircraft in 1943. It was intended for pilots who found themselves in aircraft diving at speeds close to that of sound.

A number of Allied fighter aircraft had experienced strange effects when diving at such speeds during the Second World War. Not the least of these effects had been the dangerous tendency for the controls to do the reverse of what was expected of them and for the whole aircraft to buffet and shake, sometimes to the point of structural failure. To preserve frontline fighter pilots and to investigate flight at speeds close to Mach 1 – thus forestalling any German advance in the new science – a series of high speed dives was planned.

The aircraft chosen for these investigations was the Photo Reconnaissance Spitfire (PR Mark XI) fitted with the Merlin 61 engine. Such a Spitfire was capable of climbing to 40,000 ft – high even by the standard of the subsonic jets of the mid-1980s. To achieve the highest speeds the power dive had to be started from as high as possible. For that and the reason of its relatively thin wings, the Spitfire PR Mark XI was considered a suitable aircraft for research into flight at transonic speed.

Some time in 1943, Squadron Leader Martindale, a test pilot for Rolls-Royce in civil life, found himself in a 45 degree dive from 40,000 ft. After 36 seconds from the start of the dive, descending through 29,000 ft, the Spitfire attained Mach 0.9. From about Mach 0.75 upwards some of the airflow became compressed and therefore subject to different aerodynamic laws. The Spitfire experienced increased drag, loss of lift and a tendency to pitch further nose down. Uncorrected the nose-down pitch would increase the dive angle. To prevent this the pilot would pull the stick back to apply 'up elevator'. At transonic speeds such action exposed the aircraft to another risk. Due to lack of stiffness in the tailplane and the great force of a compressed airstream on the up-going elevator, the leading edge of the tailplane could bend upwards leaving the elevator trailing in the slipstream. This resulted in the controls achieving the reverse effect of what was expected, namely pitching the aircraft further nose down. This effect is quite separate from the nose dropping due to the redistribution of the lift.

Entering the warmer atmosphere the Spitfire found itself in an environment where the speed of sound was greater. Although still travelling at roughly the same true airspeed, its speed with respect to the speed of sound (Mach number) was lower. The danger now was that the laws governing the airflow at the slower speeds would suddenly be restored. The 'up-elevator', which had maintained the dive angle could now, at the smaller Mach numbers, reassert itself with unnerving suddenness, pulling the aircraft out of the dive at such a rate that the wings might fold upwards, or flutter like a flag. There were no ejection seats in those days.

These investigations into flight at speeds close to Mach 1 would have been given immense publicity in peace-time. In the event they were cloaked in war-time secrecy and by the time the story was told, it appeared rather pedestrian compared to the rocket- and jet-propelled attempts on the sound barrier going on in the late 1940s. It is of lasting tribute to the Spitfire that it behaved better at such speeds than some of the later aircraft of supposedly more advanced aerodynamic design.

The Rolls-Royce Merlin 61 engine, which powered the PR XI, had been developed and fitted to the Spitfire Mark IX in response to a formidable new fighter fielded by the Germans in 1941: the Focke-Wulf 190. The increased performance of the Merlin 61 was largely due to the effectiveness of its supercharger. This added 70 mph to the top speed and 10,000 ft to the Spitfire's maximum altitude. In consequence it out-performed the Fock-Wulf 190.

A supercharger is a device that compresses the air before it undergoes further compression in the cylinders of a piston engine. The supercharger on the Merlin 61 engine had been refined to near perfection by a brilliant young engineer at Rolls-Royce in Derby – Stanley Hooker.

Stanley Hooker (later Sir Stanley Hooker) had been recruited in 1938 by the works manager of Rolls-Royce Ernest W. Hives (later Lord Hives of Duffield) with the somewhat enigmatic words: 'You are not much of an engineer, are you?'! Hooker's work on superchargers was soon to have great relevance in the development of the jet engine, since the centrifugal compressors of the early jet engines were similar in principle to, although much larger than, the supercharger of the Merlin. The jet engine turned out to be the most suitable power plant for continuous supersonic flight. Eleven years after his work on the Merlin supercharger, Stanley Hooker began the transformation of the Bristol Olympus engine, destined, in its most superlative version, to power Concorde.

The 'barrier' to greater speed from the Spitfire during its transonic dive was due to two effects. One was the large increase of drag it experienced as the compression waves built up at Mach 0.9; the other was the loss of thrust experienced by the propeller. The combined effect of aircraft forward speed and the turning speed of the propeller ensured that the outer portions of the propeller blades were travelling at supersonic speeds. At such speeds the propeller becomes very inefficient. Thus the Spitfire lost thrust just as its drag increased. A rocket-propelled, rather than a gravity-assisted, Spitfire might have been able to maintain Mach 0.9 for longer.

Rocket propulsion has the advantage over other kinds of propulsion in that the thrust it generates is not dependent on the forward speed of the aircraft. Nor is its thrust dependent on altitude, if anything it increases as the pressure of air around it decreases. Although rocket-propelled air-craft are spared the need of having any kind of air intakes, they suffer the greater burden of having to carry extra fuel weight in the form of liquid oxygen (or some chemical suitable for combustion with the fuel). They therefore do not give propulsion suitable for sustained flight.

Happily by 1943 there had appeared an engine which looked capable of giving sustained thrust both at subsonic and supersonic speeds. This was the jet engine. This new engine gave thrust not through a propeller, but by virtue of its high speed jet efflux. The fact that its intake might be in a supersonic airflow would be, if anything, a bonus, since the incoming air could be slowed down and therefore 'supercharged'

The Rolls-Royce Merlin engine of a Spitfire, showing the circular supercharger casing to the rear. Stanley Hooker's work on the supercharger transformed the performance of this engine; later he was to transform the Bristol Olympus jet engine

prior to entering the compressor on the engine, making the engine yet more efficient.

The inventor of the jet engine principle, Sir Frank Whittle, said that he was regarded at the time as a crazy optimist. One of his early proposals (in 1935), envisaged an engine giving 111 lb of thrust to a 2000 lb aircraft travelling at 500 mph at an altitude of 69,000 ft. It is anyone's guess what people would have said had he predicted that a 350,000 lb aircraft (including the fuel) would be capable of travelling at 1,320 mph at 55,000 ft with each of its four engines giving, at that altitude, 10,000 lb of thrust.

Jet-propelled flight became a reality in Britain in 1941 with the first flight of the Gloster-Whittle (E28/39). A Whittle engine, the Power Jets W2/700, was chosen, in 1943, as the power plant for Britain's first supersonic project: the Miles M52 (E24/43). It was hoped optimistically that the M52 would exceed 1,000 mph (about Mach 1.5) in level flight. There was a great deal of controversy over the choice of wing section for the aircraft. Thin wings, suitable for supersonic flight, seemed to be the obvious choice, but their lack of efficiency at subsonic speeds meant that the aircraft would not be able to climb to such a high altitude as one fitted with conventional wings. The higher the altitude, the higher the Mach number that could be attained in the ensuing dive. Once comfortably supersonic it was hoped that the aircraft could level off maintaining speed – engine thrust having increased to cope with the higher drag associated with supersonic flight.

The W2/700 was one of the last engines built by the Power Jets Company. Under the leadership of Frank Whittle, a small and dedicated team working in appallingly primitive surroundings near Rugby in England (Sir Stanley Hooker referred to them as Whittle's rabbit hutch) had researched, designed and built a viable jet engine. After an unsatisfactory period of liaison with the Rover company, Rolls-Royce became involved with Power Jets and, under the leadership of Stanley Hooker, set about developing and producing the jet engine in quantity.

The lineage of the modern jet engine owes far more to the early British engines than to the jet engines developed in Germany. On observing the immense length of runway required by the Me 262 (the German jet-powered fighter) on take-off, an onlooker remarked to Frank Whittle, who was also present, that it was no wonder that Hitler wanted to extend the Third Reich.

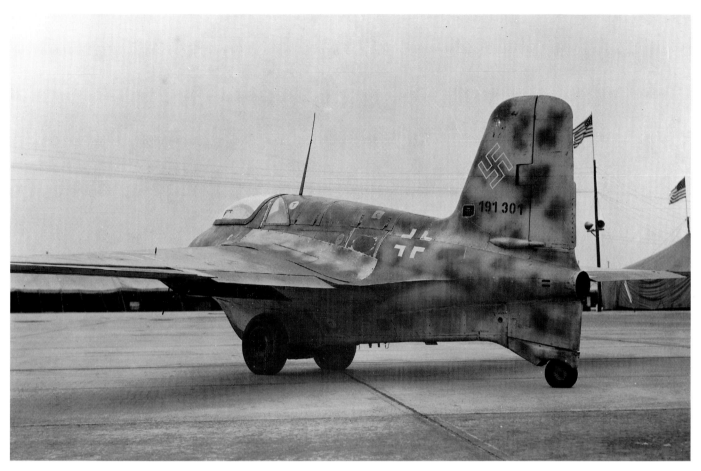

Soon it became evident that more research was needed to give sufficient thrust to the M52. The reason that the Ministry of Supply gave for the cancellation of the project in 1946, however, was that they were concerned for the safety of its pilot. In 1948, a pilotless, rocket-propelled, scaled down version of the M52 did achieve about Mach 1.4, which proved that its planform with straight wings could cope with supersonic flight. However, at the end of the Second World War, British design was influenced by swept wings which gave better performance at both supersonic and high subsonic speeds.

Before the outbreak of the Second World War a German scientist, Professor Adolf Büsemann, had published findings that suggested that swept wings would perform better than straight wings in supersonic flight. One significant reason for this is that the shock waves generated at the nose of an aircraft miss the wing tips if these are swept back. Thus there is not the added complication of an interference between wings and shock waves. Astonishingly these findings, freely available to all, went unnoticed.

Equally remarkable was the failure of the Allies to understand why the wings were

swept on the rocket-propelled German fighter (the Messerschmitt Me 163 – Komet). The Komet was a tailless swept-winged interceptor, which was very fast, achieving Mach 0.8 (about 550 mph) for short periods. The Allies believed that its speed could be ascribed to its being rocket-propelled. The reason for the swept wings was thought to be so that adequate control could be retained in pitch (the control of the longitudinal angle of the fuselage about itself). Though both beliefs were partly correct, what was not understood was that swept wings allowed the aircraft to fly at speeds closer to Mach 1, since the increase in drag was delayed until these higher speeds were reached.

From the description of the Spitfire tests, it will be remembered that some of the air becomes supersonic over an aircraft even though that aircraft is travelling subsonically. It is the portion of the supersonic airflow which causes the drag rise.

Thick wings experience this transonic drag rise at lower Mach numbers than thin wings. Wings must support the weight of the aircraft and have within them some space to contain fuel. High speed aircraft need both strength and as much space for fuel as possible. The conflict can be resolved

The Me 163B Komet, Germany's rocket-propelled interceptor. Note the absence of a tailplane. Rocket propulsion was available for 8 to 10 minutes, giving speeds in excess of 550 mph. Its swept wings allowed flight at high subsonic Mach numbers before the transonic drag rise took effect. The planform of the D.H. 108 was somewhat similar to this aircraft by sweeping the wings either forward or back. Although the ratio of the thickness of the wing to the distance from leading to trailing edge remains constant, the sweep-back makes this ratio 'appear' smaller to the airflow. Now the air is less disturbed by the passage of the aircraft, so the aircraft can fly faster before the compression waves start to apply their drag increase. The benefit of this discovery, made by Professor Albert Betz (a German aerodynamicist), has been applied to jet-propelled airliners, virtually all of which have swept back wings.

To research flight with a swept-winged aircraft, the de Havilland company modified a Vampire, a single engined, straight-winged fighter, with its tail and fin surfaces connected via twin booms to the wings. The booms and the tail surface were removed, swept back wings fitted, and a swept fin was placed over the rear end of the fuselage. It resembled the Komet in many outward respects. The DH108 was partly intended as a research aircraft for what became the Comet airliner. At that time the philosophy among several British aircraft manufac-turers had been that it was desirable to perfect a 'flying wing' to reduce the aerodynamic drag and the extra weight caused by tailplane surfaces. Sadly, after the loss of several such aircraft, to lack of control in pitch, this philosophy had to be abandoned.

'Flying wings', as tailless aircraft were

dubbed, would have had to carry their payload within the wing. For people to stand inside the wing it would have had to have been at least 7 ft thick. The wing span would have been huge to cope with such a thickness. Furthermore without a tailplane there was no way of aerodynamically balancing wing flaps. Without flaps either the landing speed would have had to have been very fast or the wing too big for efficient cruise. It would thus have been an uneconomic proposition – the de Havilland Comet had a tail!

Two other British aircraft design philo-sophies had their origins in the immediate post-war era. One was to produce a wing capable of sustaining laminar flow. Hitherto the flow of air over a wing had always been impeded by that little turbulent layer of air close to the wing known as the boundary layer. Laminar flow control promised a very marked reduction in aerodynamic drag.

The other philosophy was the notion that the aerodynamic drag associated with the engines and intakes could be reduced by placing the engine air intakes at the wing roots feeding air to engines that were 'buried', as on the Comet 4, rather than podded, as on the Boeing 707.

The laminar flow concept failed largely because it seemed impossible to retain a completely clean wing. Even a squashed insect, acquired during take-off, upset the laminar flow. Removal of the boundary layer

The D.H. 108, Britain's first transonic swept winged aircraft. Control in roll and pitch on aircraft without tailplanes has to be achieved through the surfaces on the trailing edge of the wing. John Derry exceeded the speed of sound in this aircraft (VW 120)–the first British aircraft to do so

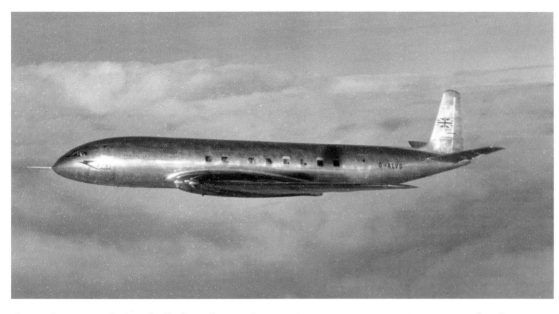

The de Havilland Comet 1, Britain's great leap forward in the post-war aviation era. Stresses at the right angular corners of the windows were higher than predicted; hence the metal fatigue that led to fatal crashes. But for the accidents de Havilland might have retained their world lead in jet airliner construction

through minute holes drilled in the surface of the wing was another solution, though rather impractical, at least in those days. However, laminar flow control was put forward again in the mid-1980s as a means of reducing drag on an Advanced Supersonic Transport (AST).

The presence of a boundary layer can be readily observed on a car windscreen during rain. Even when driving at 70 mph the smaller drops remain stationary. The larger ones which protrude out of the boundary layer are moved by the airstream but not that quickly. It is some millimetres away from the screen that the speed of the airstream assumes its expected value.

Although the concept of buried engines worked, it was not such a satisfactory answer to the drag and weight problem as the solution developed by the Americans. For their 707, Boeing placed their engines in pods slung beneath and slightly ahead of the wing, on pylons. The engine intakes benefitted from a clean airflow not disturbed by the unpredictable behaviour at the junction of wing and fuselage. Furthermore the distribution of the engine weight to the wings meant that this part of the total weight did not have to be borne through the wing root. Thus this part was lighter too.

The de Havilland Comet 4. The windows have rounded corners following experience with the Comet 1. The engines are buried at the wing roots—a philosophy preferred in Britain to the underslung pods chosen by Boeing and other US manufacturers. The pods outboard on the wings are fuel tanks

This advantage does not favour aircraft with rear fuselage mounted engines.

In 1948, John Derry, Chief Test Pilot of de Havilland, became, more by accident than by design, the first pilot in Britain to exceed Mach 1, in a DH108 during a test flight investigating transonic flight. Whilst attempting to recover from a dive at Mach 0.97, his aeroplane exceeded the vertical and achieved Mach 1.02. He was lucky to survive. Geoffrey de Havilland Jnr, son of the founder of the firm had been killed in a DH108 almost exactly two years earlier probably having experienced similar very severe oscillations in pitch.

By the early 1950s data had been acquired which would make the next steps in supersonic flight slightly easier. The first aim then was to build a jet fighter capable of intercepting the mammoth Russian nuclear bombers which were under development, and were capable of cruising between 30,000 and 40,000 ft at around Mach 0.8.

The fighter had to have an excellent rate of climb and at least double the bomber's speed for a successful interception long before the bomber could reach its target. The second aim was to build a supersonic bomber which, because of its speed, would itself be very difficult to intercept.

Long range supersonic flight, however, was going to be much more difficult to achieve than the short duration dash required of an interceptor. But should a bomber become a reality then a transport derivative could follow, such was the pattern generally established during the 50 years of aircraft development. But as far as the development of an SST was concerned, the introduction of missiles even capable of intercepting supersonic bombers at high altitude was to upset this evolutionary pattern. The SST would have to be developed almost in its own right.

The Formative Phase

The Fairey Delta 2. Fairey believed that the delta wing with no tail was the optimum solution for a supersonic aircraft. Peter Twiss achieved a new world air speed record of 1,132 mph in the FD2 in March 1956. Another version of the FD2 (BAC 221) appeared with wings modified to the 'Ogee' planform to research separated airflow on an aircraft with a greater speed range than the HP 115 for the Concorde project

Prompted by the preponderance of designs for supersonic interceptor aircraft that appeared in the early 1950s people began to wonder whether a civil supersonic transport (SST) could one day be a possibility. With London to New York flight times being of the order of 18 hours and more, especially against headwinds and with refuelling stops, the idea of doing the same journey in a fifth of the time must have seemed preposterous.

Nevertheless Sir Arnold Hall, director of the Royal Aircraft Establishment (RAE) Farnborough in the early 1950s, asked Morien Morgan, already involved with the Advanced Fighter Project Group, to chair a small committee to look into the possibility of building a civil supersonic transport. The reported findings, in 1954, suggested that it

might just be possible to fly 15 passengers from London to New York at Mach 2 in an aircraft with an all up weight of 300,000 lb (136,000 kg). For comparison Concorde carries 100 passengers (up to 128 with reduced space between seat rows) over that range with an all up weight (maximum take-off weight including the passengers and the fuel) of 408,000 lb (185,000 kg). The envisaged 15-seater SST was based on the design of the Avro 730 supersonic bomber project that was cancelled in 1957. It had thin unswept wings with engines mounted on the wing tips. But for an SST to be economically viable, a better aerodynamic shape would have to be devised.

Such a shape did appear with dramatic impact, in the form of the British Fairey Delta 2. On 10 March 1956 Peter Twiss

(Chief Test Pilot of Fairey Aviation) exceeded the previous world airspeed record, held by the American Col. Haynes in a F100 Super Sabre, by the handsome margin of 310 mph. A reheated Rolls-Royce Avon RA5 turbojet propelled the FD2 at the astonishing speed of 1,132 mph (Mach 1.7).

In November 1956 the Supersonic Transport Aircraft Committee (STAC) was formed, chaired by Morien Morgan, one of the greatest proponents for civil supersonic flight. Hearing evidence from 17 interested bodies, comprising the aircraft industry, airlines and ministries, its conclusions were reported in 1959. The result was Concorde which ten years later made its maiden flight.

Contributors to its success were the FD2 and the P1, both offsprings of Morien Morgan's Advanced Fighter Project group which had been formed in 1948. The success of these two aircraft banished the notion of some kind of intractable barrier at Mach 1, the speed of sound. It is interesting to look at the different design philosophies.

Both designers produced a different planform: the P1 with swept wings and a tailplane, while the FD2 a delta wing without a tail. Tailless designs had encountered many problems, as exemplified by Geoffrey de Havilland's experience in the DH108, hence English Electric wanted to ensure stability and control through use of a

tail surface, especially for flight in the tricky transonic range. Fairey believed, however, that a 60 degree delta with powerful trailing edge control surfaces would provide a stable aircraft throughout this range. After all, experience had pointed to the fact that tail surfaces were a major source of aerodynamic buffet at transonic speeds – why run this risk by having a tail at all?

As it turned out both designs were supremely successful. In different ways both contributed to Concorde's eventual success: the FD2, because it was converted into the modified delta shape that was to be applied to Concorde; the P1, because a great deal was learned about the variable exhaust nozzle on the Rolls-Royce Avon engine, a necessary device for the efficient use of a variable thrust reheat system. It is the variable exhaust nozzle system on the Olympus engine, as fitted to Concorde, which ekes out every last remaining ounce of thrust and fuel economy from the jet efflux both with and without reheat.

'Reheat', or 'after-burner' as it is known in the United States, is a device which can be fitted to the rear of the main jet engine, within the exhaust duct, to give an extra 'push' to the aircraft. It consists of a ring from which fuel may be burned in the engine exhaust gases, which still has sufficient oxygen in it to support combustion, prior to

P1 Lightning. The tail surface can be clearly seen. The English Electric designers considered that inclusion of a tail would give the stability and control required for supersonic flight provided it was positioned away from the wake of the wing. The exhaust nozzles of the two Avon engines are mounted one above the other. The nozzles could vary the area of the exit orifice—wide open with full reheat in use, and diminishing with intermediate amounts of reheat. Perfection of variable jet nozzles was essential before a commercial SST could become a reality

The buckets or secondary nozzles on Concorde. The left-hand picture shows the nozzle in its divergent position as it would be in supersonic flight. The right-hand picture shows the nozzle as it would be for take-off, the gap allowing ambient air to break up the boundary to the jet efflux making it less noisy. For their position to give reverse thrust, see page 104

Opposite, top *Sir Barnes Wallis with a model of Swallow. Although the cockpit and undercarriage have been extended for this photograph the wings are in the fully swept position for supersonic flight – a combination that would not have been found in practice. Surrounding Sir Barnes are examples of his earlier engineering efforts including bombs, airships, the Wellington bomber and geodetic construction*

Inset *A polymorphous photograph of Swallow showing the extent of the variable geometry. Note that the engine pairs on the wingtips were to have been hinged. There was no fin*

*See appendix (page 119).

its leaving via the exhaust nozzle. As the velocity of the jet efflux is so much greater with reheat on, the exhaust nozzle must vary in area to accommodate two situations. On the FD2 the reheat was either on or off, thus the exhaust nozzle only had the two positions – wide open or open. On the P1 the reheat was variable so the exhaust nozzle had to be variable as well. On the Olympus 593, as fitted to Concorde, not only is there a variable nozzle to accommodate the reheat, but there is a secondary nozzle which, amongst other things, forms a divergent duct for efficiency during the supersonic cruise. Furthermore the primary nozzle area varies continually, even without reheat, thus keeping the Olympus engine constantly in tune*.

The Supersonic Transport Aircraft Committee (STAC) met regularly from November 1956 until March 1959. Among its recommendations was one which strongly favoured building a long-range SST to carry 150 passengers from London to New York non-stop with a cruising speed of not less than Mach 1.8. There was also a recommendation for the construction of a shorter range SST to cruise at Mach 1.2. The committee regarded cruising speeds approaching Mach 3 as feasible, but technically difficult due to the heating effect discussed in the Preface. At Mach 3 the highest temperature experienced by the fuselage is around 335°C (635°F) thus not only is it much more difficult to keep the occupants cool, but the skin has to be made from the more expensive alloys of titanium and perhaps even from stainless steel. The cheaper and

well tested aluminium alloy, although highly satisfactory at temperatures up to 130°C (265°F), does not cope with temperatures of over 300°C (572°F) at all. A Mach 3 version was regarded by the STAC as a possible second generation SST.

Between London and New York a cruising speed of Mach 3, compared to Mach 2, would reduce the total journey time by about 40 minutes, about 20 per cent. The real gain of a Mach 2 airliner was that it could more than double the speed of the current subsonic airliners, which were designed to cruise at just above Mach 0.8. Any economic gains associated with the yet quicker journey times made possible at a speed of Mach 3 would be more than wiped out by the fact that a Mach 3 SST would cost disproportionally more to build. Development costs were put at £75–£95m for the Mach 1.8 SST and £50–£80m for the slower shorter range versions, at 1959 values. It was considered that they would cost about 50 per cent more to operate than a similarly-sized subsonic aircraft.

Following the recommendations of the STAC, feasibility studies were commissioned by the Ministry of Defence, then headed by Duncan Sandys. Bristol produced studies of an SST with a conventional fuselage and slender delta wings, but Hawker Siddeley provided a study for an integral layout – a slender delta with a longitudinal swelling in which would be housed the passengers – virtually a slender delta flying wing.

Duncan Sandys' somewhat infamous defence White Paper in 1957 had put a temporary halt to the development of manned military aircraft in Britain (including the Avro 730 supersonic bomber) in favour of missiles. So a rather stunned aircraft industry must have welcomed the opportunity to research and possibly build an SST. By 1959, when Duncan Sandys had commissioned the feasibility studies for an SST, plans for the new British Supersonic Tactical Strike Reconnaissance Aircraft – the TSR2 – had been unveiled. However, in 1966 Britain's Labour government cancelled – among other aircraft – the TSR2. To quote Sir Stanley Hooker on British military aviation policy: 'We were in, we were out, then we were in again and finally out. It was more like a boat race than a policy.'

Among other designs which were also put forward at about this time was the Barnes Wallis Swallow. This consisted of an aircraft in which variable sweep had been taken to the extreme. The engines, outboard on the wings, were hinged and could be used for stability and control in place of aerodynamic surfaces. Furthermore their movement with the wing sweep contributed to the balance of the aircraft. Concorde retains aerodynamic balance at different speeds by moving the fuel to change the centre of gravity.

An 'arrow' planform is attractive because it is very efficient aerodynamically at supersonic speeds. To keep the drag down on Swallow, the pilots would have had a retractable cockpit. Studies for advanced supersonic transports make use of the 'arrow' planform; but without recourse to variable geometry, the 'arrow' cannot be so marked as the one on Swallow. In the un-

entrance lobby

fuel

'A'

Typical section ('A'-'A')

150 passenger cabin

fuel

'A'

landing configuration

entrance lobby

The slewed-wing proposal from Handley Page. Runways would have had to have taken on different proportions if this 1961 idea had taken root!

23

The HP 115 in flight near Farnborough. This slender delta aircraft proved that a separated airflow could give lift at slow speeds. It first flew in August 1961. Its success paved the way for Concorde by showing that complex high lift devices for slow speed flight would not be necessary for slender deltas

unpalatable fact remains that there is a drag rise as Mach 1 is exceeded. In fact the L/D drops, on Concorde, from about 12 at Mach 0.95 to 7.5 at Mach 2. How then was the future SST going to have enough range to cross the Atlantic?

Happily jet-engine efficiency can be designed to improve with speed, more than compensating for the loss of aerodynamic efficiency. The projected SST was expected therefore to travel further (or at least as far) on a gallon of fuel at its supersonic cruising speed as it could at its subsonic cruising speed, expected to be in excess of Mach 0.9. This fortunate state of affairs is brought about because the efficiency of the turbojet engine is very much enhanced if the air is precompressed prior to engine entry. At speeds in excess of Mach 1.4 sufficient precompression can be arranged to occur inside the intake system where the air is slowed – hence compressed – to about half

According to some commentators the cost of developing Concorde was increased by one third due to its being a collaborative project. There were two production lines – one at Bristol (Filton) in England, and the other at Toulouse in France. Duplication of jigs and tools were two elements in this process, whilst transporting pieces made in France to Britain and vice-versa was another. Here the 'Guppy' is being loaded with a British built tail-fin and tail-cone for transport to Toulouse. Airbus Industrie (consortium of four countries) were the benefactors of the collaborative experience gained from the Concorde project

Opposite The number 4 engine intake on a Concorde. The two moveable 'ramps' can be clearly seen inside the top of the box. The extent of the movement on the forward one (labelled 'DO NOT USE . . .') can be clearly seen on the vertical dividing wall between this intake and its neighbour (to the right of this picture) in the form of 'rubbing' marks. Correct positioning of the ramps to focus the shock wave on the intake's lower lip was fundamental to engine efficiency in supersonic flight. During subsonic flight the ramps are raised, as shown here See appendix (page 119)

the speed of sound before it reaches the engine. Nobody doubted that the intake system would need some kind of variable 'throat' so that it could cope efficiently with various speeds and especially those in excess of Mach 1.5. Since engine efficiency improves with speed up to Mach 3, there was a great incentive to go as fast as the kinetic heating of the structure would allow – Mach 2.2 appeared the most attractive speed if a well-tried and tested aluminium alloy were used.

However, Mach 2.04, which reduced the maximum temperature from 156°C to 127°C (313°F to 261°F), was ultimately chosen since the lower temperature gave less of a problem with the oil and fuel.

By the late 1950s, it was realised, tantalisingly, that aerodynamic and thermo-dynamic development had progressed far enough to allow an SST to become a reality. The question now became: would disap-pointments with the performance of British civil aviation spur Government and In-dustry into turning the theory of a paper dart into a practical SST?

British civil aviation in the years after the Second World War had hoped to equal or better anything the Americans could pro-duce. It was true that two major projects had been abandoned – the Princess Flying Boat and the Bristol Brabazon. But on the credit side the pure jet de Havilland Comet 1 and the turbo-prop Vickers Viscount were about to appear. At Bristol another potential world beater, the turbo-prop Britannia was also taking shape.

The Britannia, it was hoped, would replace most long-range piston-propelled airliners. The engine chosen to power the Britannia was the Proteus. Originally de-signed to fit within the wing of the Brabazon, it had an air intake arrangement which caused the air to turn through 180 degrees before entering the engine. At 20,000 ft in the moist air found over the tropics ice formed at the 180 degree elbow causing the engine to flameout (stop) on an early Britannia. Fears of a similar, if not worse problem over the Atlantic brought matters to a head. However, the moisture content over the Atlantic at 20,000 ft is not nearly as great as it is over the tropics. According to Sir Stanley Hooker a relatively easy modification would have sufficed. Nevertheless for worldwide operations a total cure had to be found. In the end a system of igniter plugs solved the problem and BOAC accepted the Britannia – some two years late – and just in time to be overtaken by the jets on the North Atlantic, notably the Boeing 707. Instead of 180 only 80 Britannias were sold, and a jet-powered version of the Britannia was beyond the

The Bristol Britannia. The big British hope of the 1950s. Icing problems on the Bristol Proteus engines delayed its entry into service. Too soon it was overtaken by the long-range jet airliners. Its sales were further jeopardised by the appearance of the Vickers Vanguard–another four-engined turboprop airliner of similar size

resources of Bristol. On top of this, the British Aircraft Industry, lacking direction, had been allowed to build a competitor to the Britannia, the turbo-prop Vanguard. Each whittled down the sales of the other.

The designers of the medium-range jet-powered Comet 4 had, by 1958, overcome the devastating problem experienced with its direct forerunner the Comet 1. The corners of the windows had not been made strong enough to withstand metal fatigue with the result that three Comet 1s had experienced explosive decompression in flight. This salutary lesson caused the designers of Concorde to proceed with caution in every field and not least in the area of aircraft structure. The Comet 4 inaugurated the first transatlantic jet passenger service in October 1958 – two weeks before the Boeing 707.

It had been galling for Sir George Edwards, Chairman of Vickers, that BOAC had been allowed, by the British Government, to purchase the Boeing 707 from America in 1956. In the previous year, BOAC

and the RAF had turned down the British equivalent to the 707 – the Vickers VC7 (V-1000 in its military form). Based on the Vickers Valiant bomber, it had engines buried in the inboard section of the wing with intakes at the wing roots. The VC7 was scrapped, to be replaced by the Vickers VC10.

The Vickers VC10, with its clean wing and four rear-mounted engines, was originally conceived as an airliner capable of operating from high altitude airfields on hot days over the old 'empire' routes. Later its range was increased to compete with the Boeing 707. Although it was beloved by passengers as soon as it appeared in 1962, it was too late to sell in large quantities – the Boeing 707 had got in first. It typified the frightful dichotomy into which the relationship between the British Government, the nationalised carriers (BOAC and BEA) and the airline industry had fallen. The Government, according to Sir Basil Smallpeice (Managing Director of BOAC from 1956–1963), had expected BOAC to support the British Aircraft Industry by buying British aircraft it did not want and then having to bear some of the financial burden incurred during the final stages of the development of the new aircraft. At the same time BOAC was expected to pay the Government a fixed rate of interest on the capital borrowed. It was galling to BOAC that a large quantity of that capital, in 1957, had had to be spent on acquiring 10 DC7Cs to fill the gap caused by the late delivery of the Britannia 312. Thus BOAC regarded the VC10 with a great deal of caution, fearing that the Government would force them to have a large number of VC10s they simply did not want. In the end some kind of compromise was reached, but not without acrimony.

Forewarned is forearmed. Sir Basil Small-peice and Sir Matthew Slattery of BOAC made it very clear to the British Government in 1960 that although they would be delighted to assist with any future SST, this would be at no financial risk to the airline and no orders would be placed unless the SST made economic sense. In the end the Government agreed to underwrite that risk.

It is true that there had been one British success – the short-haul Vickers Viscount, with sales exceeding 400. However, by the late 1950s and early 1960s, in the words of Sir Stanley Hooker, 'We've lost in the civil market to the Americans. Now these Boeing 707s and DC8s cannot possibly last for more than about ten years. Therefore in order to collar our fair share we must look towards building a supersonic airliner with a European partner.'

A Concorde model painted in BOAC livery. By the time it made its first commercial flight, BOAC (Overseas) had merged with BEA (European) to become British Airways. The VC10s in the background at Heathrow represent the last large all British airliner, and barely 50 were built. Britain's failure to export subsonic airliners was instrumental in its decision to develop a supersonic one

Agreement with France

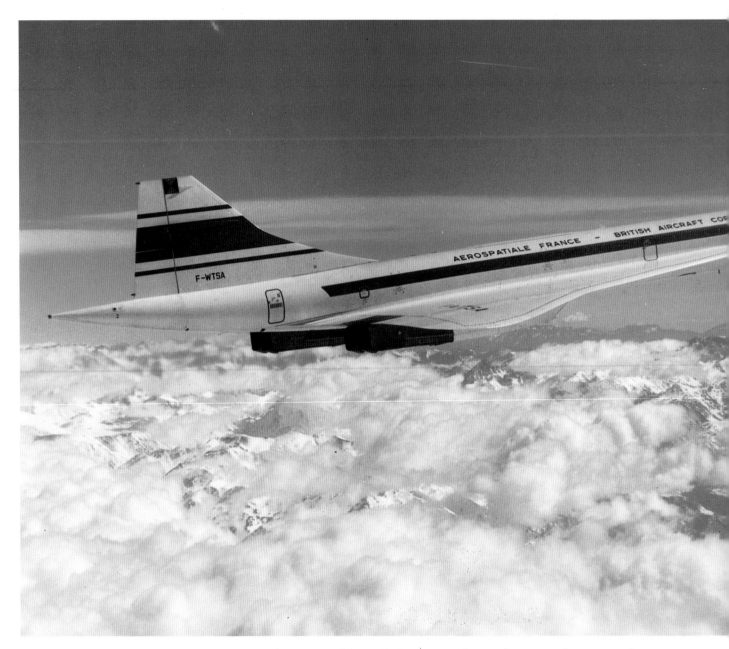

By 1961, Britain had convinced herself that it was both highly desirable and technically possible to build an Atlantic range (3,700 statute miles) SST. There was one piece of the jigsaw missing, however; could a suitable partner be found to share the large cost of such a project? The right choice of partner, it was hoped, would lead not only to a successful SST but to co-operation in a host of other fields. A European partner, for instance, might pave the way for Britain's entry into the Common Market. At that time Russia and America were pouring millions into the exploration of space, without, apart from technical advance, any prospect of financial return. An SST promised technical advance and a financial return, the latter largely on the grounds that speed had always attracted customers.

Partnership with an American company was considered. But the Americans were more interested in Mach 3 designs. Such speeds had already been ruled out by the British designers on account of the kinetic heating problem.

The only European country with the

ability to undertake such a project in the early 1960s was France. France had had to rebuild its once proud aircraft industry from the ashes of the Second World War. She was, in 1960, one of the few nations – with

Russia, the United States, Sweden, Britain and Canada – to have designed, built and tested supersonic aircraft. Nevertheless the French Aircraft Industry would benefit enormously from Britain's technical know-how which had been enhanced rather than destroyed by the Second World War. As it turned out, Britain was to benefit from France's determination to see the project through.

Starting with the straight-winged Trident, first flown in 1953, France had built a series of supersonic research aircraft. It was the Trident which on one occasion caused some concern in the echelons of the British Radar Warning System. Charles Burnet (BAe Weybridge) who witnessed the incident said: 'One evening in the late 1950s a worried controller phoned Boscombe Down to find out if there were any test aircraft airborne from there at that time. Apparently a target had been detected flying down the Channel from the east at over 1,000 mph – it turned out to be the French Trident!' This aircraft was powered by two wing tip-mounted turbojets and a rocket unit in the fuselage.

After this came the delta-winged Gerfault which was capable, in 1954, of exceeding Mach 1 by use of a turbojet alone – without reheat or rocket assistance. But most spectacular of the French research aircraft was the Nord Griffon. It had a propulsion unit which consisted of a turbojet within a huge outer casing. This outer casing formed a ramjet. The turbojet engine was used for slow speed flight and for starting the ramjet. The Griffon achieved Mach 1.85 in 1957 (about 1,240 mph).

Ramjets work on the principle that due to the high forward speed, usually above Mach 1.5, there is sufficient natural compression of the air to supplant the rotating compressor of a turbojet. No compressor means no need for a turbine to drive the compressor hence no moving parts. Air entering the intake becomes compressed, is then heated by the burning fuel giving thrust to the engine as it accelerates out of the propelling nozzle. A ramjet does not give efficient propulsion until speeds of around Mach 4 are reached.

Many missiles are propelled by ramjets, but only once they have achieved a suitable speed, usually gained from a rocket engine. Concorde travels too slowly to benefit from ramjet propulsion.

On the civil side the French had some success with the subsonic twin-engined Sud-Est Caravelle airliner. Its nose section was in fact the same as the British de Havilland Comet's. There was a lot of collaboration. Incidentally Concorde was to inherit, via this lineage, the triple hydraulic system labelled blue, green and, as a backup, yellow, which was originally fitted to the Comet.

Concurrent with the Nord Griffon were the swept-winged Mysteres and the delta-winged Mirage fighters. The next logical step for Sud Aviation, as it had become by 1961, was to investigate the possibility of

Concorde 02 – the French-constructed pre-production aircraft F-WTSA displaying both makers' names against an Alpine backdrop. By the time this picture was taken Sud Aviation had become Aerospatiale. Each country was to operate the aircraft that it had constructed. Note the extended tail cone compared to the prototypes and British pre-production Concorde 01. Every minor improvement was vital in order to achieve the design range and payload of at least Paris to Washington. The greater the fineness ratio (length to maximum diameter) the better the lift to drag ratio (about 7½ on Concorde at Mach 2, although 10 or 11 is desirable in a successor). Keeping fineness ratio high on a design with a shorter fuselage compromises internal volume, a fact that would militate against a smaller supersonic business jet

The Sud Aviation Caravelle. This successful French airliner had two rear-mounted engines. The nose owed its lines to the de Havilland Comet, as can be clearly seen

building an SST. Sud Aviation had been formed from Sud-Est, run by George Hereil, the original proposer of the Caravelle, and Sud Ouest.

Accordingly, at the Paris Air Show of June 1961 there appeared a model of a slender delta SST called the Super Caravelle. Although never built, it was designed to carry a payload of 70 passengers over 2,000 miles.

The Super Caravelle was thus not to have transatlantic range. In fact there was to be some wrangling between the British and French over this question of range. The British, in spite of a mild flirtation with an 'M-winged' medium range Mach 1.2 aircraft, had never considered it worthwhile to build anything with less range than London (or Paris) to New York. The Super Caravelle bore a remarkable resemblance to the BAC 223, the latest proposal from Archibald Russell, technical director of Bristol Aircraft which, by late 1961, had become part of the British Aircraft Corporation (BAC). (Included in the merger were Bristol Aeroplane Co Ltd, English Electric Aviation Ltd, builders of the P1 Lightning, Hunting Aircraft Ltd and Vickers-Armstrong (Aircraft) Ltd, builders of the VC10).

The BAC 223 study had followed a proposal for a larger version – the Bristol Type 198 which had been considered too ambitious to gain Ministry approval.

The Type 198 design had been originally submitted as one of the feasibility studies which had followed the recommendations of the STAC. With transatlantic range at a cruise speed of Mach 2.2, it was to have had six Olympus engines in a bank on top of the wing under the fin. The projected all up weight was to be 385,000 lb, with a passenger load of 132. Concorde turned out to be only four per cent heavier with a similar load carrying ability and four Olympus engines of increased thrust instead of the original six.

The BAC 223 on the other hand, although still with transatlantic range, had a proposed weight of 270,000 lb and was to be powered by four under-wing mounted Olympus engines. This question of size as well as range was already causing much controversy. A great deal of unnecessary expense was incurred building tools and jigs for designs that were not produced.

Duncan Sandys, perceiving the political and economic advantages of collaboration between France and Britain, had encouraged Sir George Edwards, Chairman of the new BAC, to explore the possibilities of co-operation with his French opposite number, Georges Hereil of Sud Aviation. At first, there did not appear to much of a basis for co-operation due to the differing range philosophies. So discussions centred around collaboration on a common engine, on systems, electrics and hydraulics.

To achieve better coordination, the French Minister of Transport and Britain's Minister of Aviation met in September 1961. This resulted in a firm directive to the participating firms to resolve their differences. But collaboration proved more difficult for the airframe manufacturers, whose ideas on range were becoming more entrenched, than for the engine manufacturers. There was only one engine that could sensibly be used for both the medium and long haul SST: the Bristol-Siddeley Olympus.

Bristol Aero-engines had persevered privately with the Olympus in spite of Government policy which had decreed, in 1957, that there would be just the one large engine programme, centred on the Rolls-Royce Conway engine. Had it not been for the wisdom and foresight of Sir Reginald Verdon-Smith, Chairman of the Bristol Aeroplane Company, there would have been no engine immediately available and suitable for an SST.

There followed more meetings between

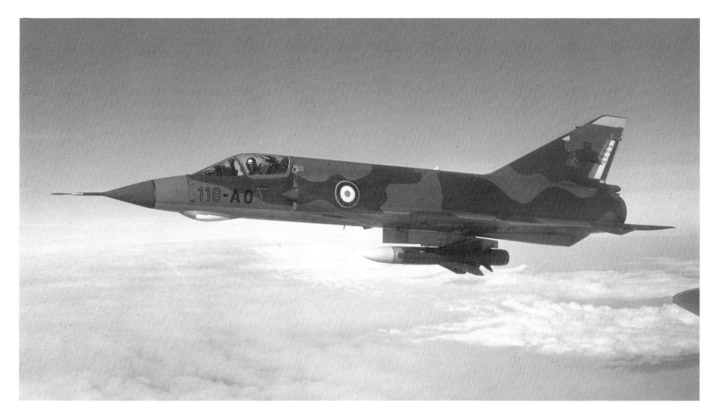

the respective ministers to encourage collaboration. There was little result at first, other than the making of a few conciliatory gestures – the building of the tail section of the Super VC10 was subcontracted out to a Sud Aviation subsidiary.

Then in 1962 de Gaulle came to power in France. General Andre Puget replaced Georges Hereil, while in Britain Julian Amery became the Minister of Aviation. These changes propelled the two countries into an agreement with one another. De Gaulle saw this as a way of improving the French Aircraft Industry while Puget, unlike Hereil, was on the same wavelength as George Edwards; Amery was to seal this concord with an unbreakable treaty.

Just before the signing of the treaty the Americans became perturbed by the progess being made in the field of SSTs in Europe. Accordingly Eugene Black, ex-Chairman of the World Bank and a

The Mirage III. The French pursued the delta planform after the British success with the FD2. The Mirage has been a great success for the French aircraft industry

The medium range M-winged Mach 1.2 proposal from Armstrong Whitworth. The cone at the nose would have kept the nose shock wave clear of the wings. Area ruling, apparent where the fuselage is waisted, was intended to keep the drag down. Concorde was not quite long enough to have required area ruling

The Rolls-Royce/SNECMA Olympus 593–610 engine, powerplant for Concorde. Between 50,000 and 60,000 ft at Mach 2 it is the world's most efficient aero engine, with more than 40 per cent thermal efficiency. With re-heat on take-off it delivers over 38,000 lb of thrust, during the supersonic cruise around 10,000 lb

Concorde's family tree. The Super Caravelle and BAC 223 were only design studies. The Type 221 was a modification of the FD2

SYSTEMS RESPONSIBILITIES
BAC
Electrics
Oxygen
Fuel
Engine instrumentation
Engine controls
Fire
Air conditioning distribution
De-icing

AEROSPATIALE
Hydraulics
Flying controls
Navigation
Radio
Air conditioning supply

British
French

Engines & TRA nozzles – Rolls-Royce/SNECMA

The distribution of responsibilities for the manufacture of Concorde. Broadly the breakdown between France and Britain was 60:40 for the airframe and 40:60 for the engine

prominent and influential individual in the US corridors of power, attempted to dissuade Julian Amery from continuing with his plans. According to Geoffrey Knight (one time director of BAC) in his book *Concorde the Inside Story* this merely had the effect of encouraging Amery to go ahead. The Americans were afraid that Britain's gamble was going to pay off. It turned out that Eugene Black was about to become Chairman of a high-powered committee set up to study the possibility of the United States building an SST.

On 29 November 1962 an agreement between the governments of France and Britain was signed and registered at the Hague. The agreement comprised seven articles. It included clauses about each country having equal responsibility for the project, bearing equal shares of the cost, and sharing equally the proceeds of sales. Two aircraft – a long-range and a medium-range one – were envisaged. Every effort was to be made to carry out this programme with equal attention to both the medium and long-range versions. There were to be two integrated organisations taken from British and French firms – BAC and Sud Aviation for the airframe, Bristol Siddeley and SNECMA for the engine – which were to make detailed proposals for carrying out the programme. There was no break clause. The agreement was signed by Julian Amery and Peter Thomas (Parliamentary Under-Secretary of State, Foreign Office) for the United Kingdom and G de Courcel, French Ambassador in Britain, for France.

It was the first time in history that such a collaborative organisation had been set up.

The bureaucratic machinery that was to control the project ensured three things. First that every decision was minutely and critically examined by both partners. Secondly, as a result of the first, a superior aircraft was to evolve. Thirdly, the process would take longer and cost more than if it had been organised individually or with one country having design leadership.

The first flight of the prototype was expected during the second half of 1966, while the first production aircraft was due at the end of 1968, with a Certificate of Airworthiness (C of A) being granted at the end of 1969. In the event, the first prototype flew in March 1969, and the C of A was granted in late 1975.

The development costs of the project in 1962 were put at between £150m and £170m. The division of responsibility was to be 60:40 between France and Britain on the airframe and 40:60 on the engine. For various reasons connected with inflation, devaluation of the pound, the reworking of the design in 1964 for just the long haul version and the longer time it took to complete, the project eventually cost, as we shall see, rather more!

Britain was not yet a member of the Common Market. As one commentator put it 'Concorde was conceived before the two contracting partners were joined in wedlock.' In spite of the agreement, membership of the EEC by Britain was put off a further nine years. So even this act of European unity, in the face of American aviation technology, was not enough; de Gaulle was still suspicious of Britain's special relationship with the United States.

Taking Shape

Taking Shape

An SST has to operate in an extraordinarily hostile environment. At Mach 2 it experiences a freezing wind of such force that the fuselage is heated to the boiling point of water, shock waves tear at every angle on its airframe, and all this occurs at an altitude where the atmospheric pressure is a tenth of its value at sea level. Only military aircraft flown by pilots, equipped with sophisticated oxygen supplies and wearing pressure suits, had ventured to these extremes and then usually only for minutes at a time. The SST was designed to carry ordinary airline passengers in complete comfort and safety for hours at a stretch. Could the fusion of British and French philosophies possibly produce such a craft?

Judging from the expected timescale of the project there was confidence that success would come quickly. The physics of obtaining lift throughout the speed range was understood. The loss in aerodynamic efficiency at speeds above Mach 1 would be more than compensated by the improvement in the efficiency of the intake and engine combination achievable at Mach 2. A certain amount of ingenuity would be called for in some areas – notably in the engine air intake, air conditioning and fuel systems. Novel techniques, like the redistribution of the fuel in flight to maintain the balance of the aircraft, would have to be developed.

The aircraft also would need to behave in a way that pilots had been trained to expect. A slender delta-winged aircraft with no horizontal tail surfaces behaves differently from a swept-winged aircraft with a tail. It is less naturally stable in speed – a conventional aircraft is designed so that a speed increase over the tail surface causes an extra downforce on the tail. This pitches the aircraft into a climb which, without a thrust increase, restores the speed. Also its ratio of pitch to roll is different from a conventional aircraft because of its length and small wingspan. Rather than rely on excessive training time to teach pilots new techniques it would be safer to fit the aircraft with computers to give it the feel of a conventional aircraft.

The design was revolutionary. In spite of the very best endeavours of the designers there was no way of predicting the

The full scale wooden mock-up of Concorde at Filton, England. This mock-up was used to check emergency evacuation systems as well as being an example of the appearance of the finished product for prospective purchasers

The Convair B-58 Hustler bomber. An engine failure at supersonic speeds, on this delta aircraft, was barely survivable

An Avro Vulcan with five Olympus engines. The centre one – the Olympus 593 – is shown here undergoing icing trials. Water droplets, simulating flight in cloud, were released ahead of the intake from the device beneath the nose. An unchecked build up of ice within the intake and over the first compression stages of the engine would radically affect performance. Heat applied either electrically or from hot air on vulnerable surfaces overcomes the problem

interaction of *all* the systems before the first flight of the prototypes. There might be some totally unforeseen side effect which could take years to iron out, like some quirk in the airflow affecting just one engine, necessitating a control law peculiar to that engine alone. Indeed such a problem did arise, but mercifully a simple solution was found.

Having designed a practical aircraft, it would be worthless unless it were safe.

Making the structure safe, yet light, would stretch the powers of the designers. Having built the structure it would have to be tested to limits beyond those that could be explored in flight. To achieve that full scale versions of the airframe would have to be dedicated to ground-testing. All the stresses and strains of high altitude flight would be applied to them, including the repeated heating and cooling of the airframe, experienced on each supersonic flight to at least one of them.

Very high altitude flight is advantageous to an SST since it can fly at a far lower indicated airspeed for a given true airspeed (see page 11). At 60,000 ft travelling at Mach 2, or 1,150 knots true airspeed, Concorde only 'feels' 435 knots of airspeed. Fighter aircraft have to be built with sufficient strength to withstand turbulent air at indicated airspeeds in excess of 700 knots. Such a speed, apart from being quite unnecessary for an SST, would call for a stronger and therefore heavier structure. With the very small margin available of payload weight to total weight, the SST could not be allowed to have the luxury of a high indicated airspeed limit. The indicated airspeed limit on Concorde varies with altitude, reaching a maximum of 530 knots

A full sized rig was made to check the working of Concorde's fuel system. Apart from supplying the engines, the fuel is used to move the centre of gravity rearwards during acceleration and forwards prior to landing as well as being a medium for cooling the air in the air conditioning system and cooling the engine oil

at 43,000 ft. A typical limit for a subsonic passenger jet is 350 knots (see page 122).

Off-setting the advantage of flying high is the disadvantage that the fuselage has to be made strong enough to withstand high differential pressures. To give a cabin altitude of 6,000 ft when the aircraft is at 60,000 ft requires a differential pressure approaching 11 lb per square inch (psi). Hitherto the limit for subsonic jets had been about 8 lb psi which gave them a cabin altitude of over 7,000 ft at an aircraft altitude of 37,000 ft.

Large aircraft require a multitude of systems: electrics, hydraulics, navigation, undercarriage and flying controls to name but a few. Systems fundamental to the safety of the aircraft must have back up systems. Some systems on Concorde were to have additional back up systems. For instance, Concorde is fitted with four methods of lowering the undercarriage: two of them from different hydraulic sources; one by letting it down by its own weight; and a fourth by use of compressed air.

Before passengers could be carried every conceivable combination of failures and consequent recourse to back up systems

There are four undercarriage legs on Concorde, here seen at half travel. The length of the main gear legs is governed by having to keep the rear of the engines clear of the ground at the high aircraft pitch angles associated with take-off and landing. The tail gear is there as a precaution against this eventuality. The camber on the wing (roughly the amount that the leading and trailing edges are bent downwards), can be seen from this picture. It helps to minimise the rearward movement of the centre of lift with increasing Mach number, thus the requirement to move the centre of gravity so far rearward is also minimised had to be explored. Might the warning of a failure of one system cause the pilots to take inappropriate action? Just prior to Concorde entering service it was discovered that the loss of some of the hydraulic pressure to the flying controls during the early stages of the take-off run resulted in an instruction to the pilots to abandon the take-off. This required the application of the wheel brakes, themselves requiring hydraulic pressure supplied from the source whose failure caused the take-off to be abandoned. Although hydraulic pressure to the brakes could be restored in seconds, that would be too late for an aircraft travelling at 270 ft per second: the aircraft would overrun. So an instantaneous and automatic change-over from one hydraulic supply to another had to be the solution.

Safety at the level of system failures was one thing, but would the SST be able to survive a potentially more catastrophic incident? Would it be controllable during conditions following the simultaneous failure of two engines on one side? The answer had to be 'yes'. But when the British and French prepared to join forces in 1961, experience of such incidents had not been good.

The world's first big supersonic jet was the four-engined, delta-winged American Convair B58 Hustler. It was not capable of surviving a single engine failure at Mach 2, let alone two on the same side. Even flight at other speeds was risky – a B58 crashed during a display at the 1961 Paris Airshow. Deaths of B58 crew were common occurrences in spite of their being housed in escape capsules. It would be small comfort for a Concorde passenger to think that the pilot and his crew were similarly protected while he was not!

No country had yet been called upon to award a Certificate of Airworthiness for the transport of the fare-paying public in an SST. New rules had to be introduced. Every detail of the new aircraft would suffer the expert scrutiny of the civil aviation authorities of Britain, France and, as a prospective purchaser, the United States.

There are conflicting requirements on any aircraft. On an SST such conflict is extreme: too strong and it would be too heavy; too efficient at one speed, it might be unflyable at another; highly efficient engines at Mach 2 might be noisy on take-off. Compromise and ingenuity would find solutions, but the margins were narrow. The payload to maximum take-off weight on the long range

The Concorde production line at Toulouse, France, the other line was at Filton, England. It is doubtful that any future collaborative project on the scale of Concorde would have duplicate production lines

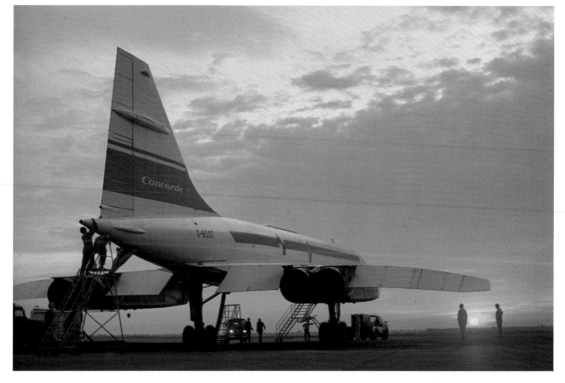

Concorde 01 – the first pre production aircraft inside the 'Brabazon' hangar at Filton, Britain. Note the shorter tail cone found on this and the two prototype Concordes, and the original secondary nozzle system visible here on number three engine. On production aircraft this was replaced by variable 'buckets'

The Concorde production line at Filton, England. Concorde 202 (G-BBDG) can be seen in the background. These hangars had originally been built for the production of the Bristol Brabazon

airliners of the 1960s was 10 per cent; the Boeing 747s of the 1970s give 20 per cent. The SST would be lucky to achieve 5 per cent over a 3,500 nm range. A small error in performance would remove the ability to carry any payload between London and New York (see page 118).

The small predicted payload to weight ratio did not daunt the supporters of the SST. The difference would be restored by the greater number of Atlantic crossings achievable by one aircraft. The price of fuel was expected to remain constant, even fall a little! The sonic boom, however, did cause concern.

An aircraft travelling at speeds above Mach 1.15, depending on atmospheric conditions, causes a double boom to be audible on the surface. Should this preclude supersonic flight over populated land, the medium-range SST espoused by the French would be a non-seller, as there are too few viable medium range routes which fly over the sea (see sonic boom propogation photograph, page 58).

In 1966 the designers hoped that two very similar SSTs would be built. The medium-range version would have space for more passengers and less fuel whilst the long-range version would reverse the mix. They discovered, however, that each design compromised the other. Coupled with thoughts about the sonic boom, this finally killed off the medium-range SST.

Nevertheless the two prototype Con-cordes 001 and 002, whose building had commenced in April 1965, could not be described as long-range SSTs. The same applied to the two pre-production Con-cordes – 01 and 02. The final production version of Concorde (serial numbers from 201 to 216) was not only a long range SST but also came very close to Archibald Russell's original specification – the Bristol Type 198. Designing, tooling and building of three different versions of Concorde added very greatly to the cost and the time spent on the project. On top of this problem, the whole project had duplicate headquarters, at Filton and Toulouse, mainly for political reasons. With hindsight it is absolutely remarkable that such a fine aircraft as Concorde could have had such a com-plicated beginning.

No less troublesome to the project were the various changes of government on the British side. No soon as one government takes over, its predecessor's activities come up for scrutiny. The Labour Government which took over from the Conservatives in 1964 was a case in point. It was only the agreement between France and Britain jointly to build an SST – an agreement that had been registered at The Hague – which prevented cancellation of the project.

Pressure had also been mounting from America for Britain to abandon various aviation projects – among them the TSR2 supersonic military aircraft. Why should the United States lend money to Britain only to

G-AXDN (Concorde 01) landing at Farnborough. Here the aircraft is at an angle to the oncoming airflow (angle of attack) of some 14°, so with the attitude (angle of the longitudinal axis of the aircraft to the horizontal) at 11°, the descent angle is 14° −11° which is 3°. This is the normal descent slope (known as the 'glideslope') to the runway. However, at this attitude the pilots would not have been able to see the runway over a nose pointed and streamlined for supersonic flight, hence the nose and visor are lowered, as shown here. Over the leading edges of the wings there is a wisp of condensation caused by the sudden decrease in air pressure (and therefore temperature) in the vortices over the wings. The use of this separated airflow to give lift over the wings is described on page 24, and further illustrated in the picture of Concorde's first landing on page 48. The markings under the port wing were to measure the extent of the build up of ice. Concorde 01 is now displayed at Duxford, near Cambridge

André Turcat in Concorde 01 F-WTSS, which became, under his command on 2 March 1969 from Toulouse, the first Concorde to become airborne. Compare the prototype with the 'production' version of the flight deck on page 82. The four 'fire levers' are placed on the central portion of the 'glare shield', whilst later versions have the automatic pilot control switches

fund aircraft projects which would compete with the American aviation industry? According to Julian Amery, the British minister who had concluded the agreement with France, the Americans had insisted that Concorde should be stopped. George Brown, the Minister of Economic Affairs of the new 1964 Labour Government denied that this was so. Following publication of Geoffrey Knight's book *Concorde the Inside Story* in 1976, Lord George Brown accused Mr Knight (in a letter to *The Times*, 7 May 1976) of getting 'almost every strand of his story wrong', although he admitted that he had not read the book. Nevertheless Geoffrey Knight later confirmed that there had indeed been US pressure against Concorde.

At industry level the story was different. From Boeing (the company chosen to build the US SST) came support for the European project. At first sight it might seem odd that a rival should support a rival, but this support was mutual. Each company felt that

if its rival was allowed to continue, then its own chances were bettered. This was borne out by the plethora of difficulties that faced Concorde as soon as the United States SST project was cancelled in 1971. Sadly much of that difficulty came from ill-informed political manoeuverers. Happily that lobby has become far better informed.

On 2 March 1969, the day before I joined BOAC, these difficulties lay in the future. On that day, André Turcat (director of Flight Test Aerospatiale) was to attempt to take Concorde 001 into the air for the first time from Toulouse. As an observer of the television coverage I can well remember the occasion. Bad weather had delayed the flight but at last Concorde 001 was lining up for take off. About 30 seconds worth of take-off run would prove whether the preceding seven years had been spent in vain; they were not, she flew. It was an amazing moment.

Only the low speed and low altitude range of the flight envelope (combination of speed and altitude at which an aircraft is allowed to fly) were to be explored on this day. Did the indications of speed and altitude correspond to those of the chase aircraft? The undercarriage was not even raised. Take-off and flight proved to be possible, but could the slender delta be made to land?

Some 35 minutes later Concorde 001 was on final approach at Toulouse, and all looked well. On touchdown, two clouds of dust and smoke were whisked from the wheels into the vortices over each wing. Maskell and Kuckemann had been right: a separated airflow had given lift even to an aircraft as big as Concorde. Though fully aware that far better pictures would be immediately available I nevertheless photographed the event from the television screen to have, as it were, a personal record of Concorde's first landing (see page 48).

Some minutes later surrounded by cameras and microphones André Turcat announced in French and English. 'The big bird flies'. Far greater men than one future

Concorde pilot could now turn their attentions to future demands, secure in the knowledge that the first hurdle had been safely surmounted.

Just over one month later the British-assembled prototype Concorde 002 took-off from Filton with Brian Trubshaw (Chief Test Pilot of BAC) at the controls. John Cochrane was the co-pilot and Brian Watts the Flight Engineer. As the flight deck is over 35 ft above the runway on main wheel touch-down, of key assistance in landing is the radio altimeter. Concorde has two radio altimeters, on this occasion both failed, so the landing at Fairford, Concorde's British test flight base (on account of its long runway), had to be done by eye.

Just under six years of testing and building were to elapse before Concorde's first commercial flight. During that time crises of all sorts presented themselves: environmental, political, technical and economic. Concorde's surviving of them all, ranks as a modern wonder of the world.

On the flight deck of Concorde 002 Brian Trubshaw (Chief Test Pilot BAC) and John Cochrane (BAC Test Pilot) – the pilots of the first test flight of 002, 9 April 1969. Note the large empty box at the centre of the instrument panel – space for a 'moving map display' which was later removed. In 1974 John Cochrane was responsible for landing 002 safely after an over-quick extension of the left main gear broke its main side stay. The gear was strengthened after this incident

First flight of 001 at Toulouse, 2 March 1969

Below G-BSST, 5,500 hours of flight testing, about four times as many as for a similarly sized subsonic aircraft, were necessary before Concorde could enter scheduled service

Opposite page Concorde 002 arriving at Fairford at the end of her maiden flight, 9 April 1969. Fairford, with its long flat runway, rather than Filton, was established as the British test base on the insistence of Brian Trubshaw

Right Concorde's first landing at Toulouse, 2 March 1969. This shot, from a black and white television screen, clearly shows the vortices etched by the smoke from the tyres on touchdown

The Other Supersonic Transports

Of the three SSTs only Concorde became successful. The swing wing B2707–200 having proved too ambitious a project, Boeing resorted, in 1969, to the 2707–300 version (shown here as a model at centre). By 1971 the US government withdrew support even for this programme. On the left is a model of the first version of the TU 144 and on the right a model of a prototype Concorde showing the original visor – fitted only to the two prototypes

The flight deck of the Boeing 747 is situated above the first class passenger cabin. The decision to put it there was so that it would be easy to convert the airliner into a freighter. This could be done by fitting a cargo door in the nose and removing the seats. Boeing believed, during the design phase of the 747 in the mid 1960s, that supersonic transports would, render their jumbos obsolete as passenger carriers, but not as freighters. They had good reason for their belief: the Concorde project had started in November 1962 and in June 1963 President Kennedy had announced that the US would develop an SST.

That announcement came after much lobbying of the President by the FAA (Federal Aviation Authority) administrator, Najeeb Halaby. He warned of dire consequences if the US were unable to build a challenger to Concorde, adding that the

President could conceivably find himself flying in a foreign aircraft. In the same way that Russian success had spurred on the US space programme, Concorde, especially after Pan Am announced its intention to buy six, catalysed the US reaction to SSTs. They would build one too.

To compensate for a late start the US SST had to be much larger and faster than Concorde. To this end a competition was planned, administered by the FAA, to look for the best airframe and the best engine. On 31 December 1966 it was decided that a Boeing design with swing wings (designated B2707–200) and powered by four General Electric engines was the aircraft to carry the US into the supersonic passenger age. The runner up in the competition had been the non-variable geometry Lockheed L-2000 – a proposal of similar shape to Concorde. Had the Lockheed version been

The Boeing 2707-200 of 1966. Note the presence of flaps and slats further complicating the engineering problems already associated with the swing wings

chosen, history might well have been very different. In April 1967 President Johnson gave the go-ahead for the next phase, a four year $1,600m prototype programme. Unlike previous US civil projects this one was to be financed on a 90:10 Government to industry ratio, changing to 75:25 for cost over-runs.

Half as long again as Concorde, the B2707-200 at 318 ft would have been the longest aircraft ever built. The design was intended to carry over 300 passengers at Mach 2.7 (about 1,800 mph) over 3,900 statute miles at altitudes up to 70,000 ft. Not only would its swing wings (fitted with conventional flaps and slats) give it a good take-off and landing performance, but they would give a higher aerodynamic efficiency at subsonic cruising speeds compared to a fixed delta design. Its maximum weight was to have been 675,000 lb (306,000 kg) almost one and three quarter times that of

Concorde. Each of the GE4 turbojet engines would have been capable of producing nearly 70,000 lb of thrust – not quite double that of Concorde. Due to the kinetic heating experienced at Mach 2.7, a titanium alloy would be required, such high temperatures (as hot as 260°C/500°F) being too great for aluminium alloys (see page 11).

By any definition it was an ambitious project and very quickly ran into difficulties. The hinge mechanism for the swing wings presented the greatest problem. For maximum effectiveness swing wings must have their pivots as close to the centreline of the aircraft as possible, since the greatest benefit of increased wing span can be so achieved. However, this interfered with the undercarriage and the positions of the engines. For it to be worth having swing wings their associated machinery must not be too heavy. By 1969 it appeared that their

History might have been different had Lockheed's proposal for an SST, the L2000, been chosen instead of Boeing's highly complex swing-wing one

The (US) General Electric GE4 turbojet engine of the late 1960s exceeded 63,000 lbs thrust on test. Four of the world's then most powerful jets would have propelled the B2707. Silencing such an engine would have been difficult. The GE90 turbofan (up to 115,000 lbs thrust) is a contender for the projected Very Large Airliner (600 tons +) of the 21st century, and with its lower jet exhaust velocity would be naturally quieter – hence the Rolls-Royce/SNECMA proposal for the Mid Tandem Fan arrangement for a Concorde successor

The Boeing 2707-200. By the time this version of Boeing's variable swept winged SST had appeared, grave doubts as to its viability were being voiced. Here a 'Canard' has appeared to overcome shortcomings in pitch control

Above *The double-jointed droop nose on this model of the Boeing 2707-200 displayed at the Boeing Museum of Flight during Concorde's visit to Seattle in November, 1984*

Opposite top *A good view of the underside of the later version of the TU 144. Compare the arrangement of the undercarriage, the intake boxes and the presence of a canard with the earlier version of TU 144*

weight might be such that no payload could be carried.

So Boeing, unable to continue with the swing-wing project, submitted another design for FAA approval. The B2707-300 was somewhat similar to Concorde but it had a more marked double-delta wing and a tailplane. The same engines and as many of the original systems as possible were to be used. This time about 250 passengers were to be accommodated and the expected range was to be about 4,200 statute miles. But with a Mach 2.7 cruising speed, a titanium alloy, as yet not finally developed, would have been necessary. In comparison to Concorde's very simple arrangement of six elevon surfaces, the B2707-300 had a tailplane as well as control surfaces on the trailing edge of the wing. As with Concorde, the design of the B2707-300 became more difficult as it progressed. By 1970 political and environmental opinion was hardening against SSTs. Their future looked uncertain.

The environmentalists found allies among the US politicans critical of government expenditure on civil programmes. Had the same politicians withdrawn financial support from environmental programmes, then there would have been no joining of forces. As it was, both parties wanted the US SST to be cancelled. Notable among the politicians was Senator William Proxmire. Among the environmentalists were groups that delighted in such names as 'The Committee for Green Foothills' and 'Friends of the Wilderness'.

On 24 May 1971 they won their victory. The Senate and the House of Representatives both voted against further funds being made available for the US SST. For a sum of money about equal to that spent by Britain on Concorde, the US aerospace industry had nothing to show but tons of paperwork. Boeing's workforce at Seattle was drastically cut. Bleak though it was for Boeing, the Concorde protagonists knew that their task was now harder. Without an American contender the full force of the environmentalists, flushed with victory, would be focused on them. Even the presence of the Soviet SST (the TU 144) would not count much in Concorde's favour. The technological mood in America, galvanised into such an intensive exploration of space by early Russian success had been assuaged by the moon landings. The TU 144 now appeared a relatively minor threat to prestige. The new creed among some in the US seemed to be: 'If you cannot beat them, then question the morality of their projects.'

In Russia nobody appeared to question the anachronism of an egalitarian state producing an aircraft suitable only for commissars. The TU 144 was not a copy of Concorde although superficially it looked very similar. It was supposed to be able to carry 121 passengers at Mach 2.35 (1,550 mph) over a distance of 4,000 statute miles – a performance which, on paper, was slightly

The first version of the TU 144 had the four separate engine intakes ducts contained within a single box. Note the absence of a canard. Although superficially similar to Concorde's wing in two dimensions, the TU 144's wing lacks the complex three dimensioned shaping found on Concorde

flying is required during conversion to Concorde, the whole conversion process taking about six months

There still remains information on Novosibirsk in the computer of the Concorde simulator at Filton. Had the TU 144 been a success, a trans-Russian route might have been possible. Note the runway lights visible through the windscreen when this picture was taken with the simulator 'pilotless' and 'frozen' on final approach

superior to that of Concorde. 'Concordski', as the TU 144 was dubbed, had a less complicated wing than her European rival. Instead of the ogival form with the curved leading edge joining the two angles of sweep-back, as on Concorde, the TU 144 was more distinctly a 'double delta'. The wing also exhibited less camber droop and twist than Concorde's. The four long engine intakes for the NK 144 turbofan engines were arranged in one box underneath the centreline but with dividing walls between them. The main gear was away from this box, retracting into a bay which protruded into blisters above and below the wing surface. There were no underfloor holds; baggage and freight were to be carried in panniers stowed between the two cabins and in a compartment to the rear over the engines.

The TU 144 however chalked up several 'firsts'. On 3 December 1968 she made her maiden flight, two months ahead of Concorde. In June 1969 Mach 1 was exceeded and in May 1969 Mach 2 was achieved. The respective dates for Concorde 001 (F-WTSS) were October 1969 and November 1970. However, there were problems with the Russian design as Sir George Edwards, Chairman on BAC, had pointed out to the Russians in 1967. The engines were in the wrong place, too close inboard; presumably they had been so positioned to make the aircraft easier to control in the event of engine failure. The engines were 'turbofans' and this would impair efficiency during supersonic cruise. The wing was not sufficiently sophisticated which would impair effectiveness and efficiency throughout the speed range.

At its appearance in the 1973 Paris Airshow, the TU 144 looked to have been radically redesigned. The pairs of engine intakes were now in two separate boxes, placing the engines further outboard, while the main undercarriage legs now retracted into a compartment within the engine intakes. A retractable 'canard' or foreplane appeared, placed above, and just to the rear of the flight deck. Extended, the canard would improve low speed flying characteristics by giving a lifting force to the front of the aircraft. This would now be countered by the elevons to the rear of the wing controlling the aircraft in pitch (and roll) going a few degrees down, thus giving 'flap' effect to the wing. Retracted, the canard would not interfere with the supersonic airflow. The Boeing 2707-200 (swing-wing)

design eventually included a canard too; but it was non-retractable and was there to assist control in pitch. To be fair, Concorde also appeared in progressively superior forms, but never with such a radical change as that exhibited by the TU 144.

Tragically the new version of the TU 144 crashed at the 1973 Paris Airshow. It appeared to be attempting to recover from a dive, but no really satisfactory explanation has been put forward for the disaster. On 26 December 1975 the TU 144, which apparently had not been modified greatly following the tragedy, entered service between Moscow and Alma-Ata, capital of Kazakstan. It carried mail and freight over this 1,800 statute mile sector and flew at about Mach 2.05, between 52,500 and 59,000 ft for much of the distance.

By 1985, if not years before, the TU 144 was out of service. There were unconfirmed reports of another accident, but such events, unless they involve foreigners, are usually cloaked in Soviet secrecy. There is no evidence to believe that the TU 144 ever achieved its design range and payload. On the contrary, it almost certainly had to use the afterburners (reheat) during cruise, and so it is unlikely that it had sufficient engine efficiency to fly transatlantic ranges.

This failure had one effect on Concorde. There had been plans for a trans-Soviet service by Concorde to Japan stopping at Moscow and Novosibirsk. With no TU 144 to take up reciprocal rights, the Soviet authorities were unlikely to approve a scheduled Concorde route over Russia. A last memorial to this plan remains. In the computer for the Concorde flight simulator at Filton there exists information about Novosibirsk, available should BA crews ever have needed training for this airfield.

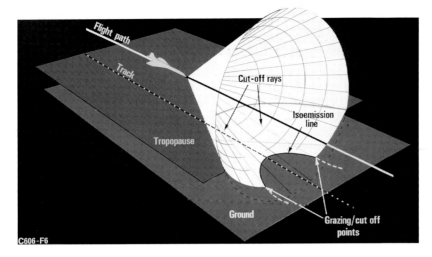

The direction of the 'ray' path of the shock wave is at right angles to the line of the wave. As the shock waves descend into the warmer air near the earth's surface their path bends concave to the sky. Thus shock waves generated by aircraft at low supersonic Mach numbers are not heard on the surface, having been refracted upwards, in a way analogous to a mirage

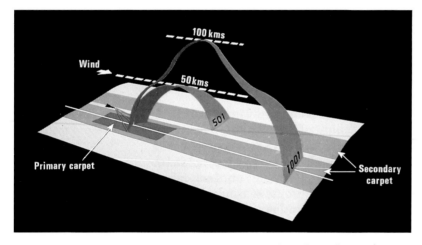

A portion of the upgoing wave can be refracted back to the surface forming a secondary boom. The guns of the western front in France, during the First World War, were heard faintly in certain places in England, on still evenings, further from them, than in others, closer to them, due to this effect. During the winter when the upper westerly winds are stronger, eastbound Concordes decelerate through Mach 1 further from a 'boom sensitive' coast to minimise this effect

Under some conditions the shock wave can bounce, as shown here. The amount of energy returning to earth from these effects is tiny. Loose windows can sometimes be rattled by them, as by a gust of wind. The reflected and refracted boom is usually inaudible unless the ambient noise is virtually zero

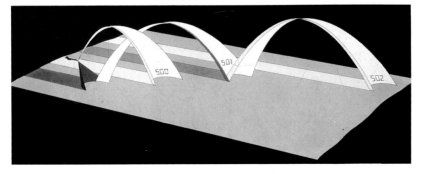

'boom sensitive' land. Where there was no way round, the higher subsonic cruising speed of an SST would give it a small edge, about 100 mph, over the majority of subsonic aircraft. Most Concorde routes do include a small proportion of flight at Mach 0.95.

On the question of solar flares, Concorde is fitted with a radiation meter. The usual dosage rate of cosmic radiation over the latitudes between London and New York at 55,000 ft is around 1 millirem per hour (about twice that found at 35,000 ft). Solar flares could cause the dosage rate to exceed 50 millirem per hour. In every case so far, the presence of radiation from a solar flare has been forecast since the flare can be seen about a day before the associated radiation reaches the earth. If radiation were encountered Concorde would descend to an altitude where, shielded by more atmosphere above, the radiation rate is lower. A survey used in 1976 showed that such evasive action would have had to have taken place five times during the previous 39 years. No radiation warnings from space have been received on Concorde during the first 10 years of commercial operation. Although the dosage rate on a subsonic aircraft is half as much, the occupants experience the effect for twice as long, thus receiving a similar quantity to that received by a Concorde passenger. Furthermore subsonic flights over the poles, where the radiation is higher, expose the aircraft's passengers to more radiation.

Placing this all in context, an individual's dose of radiation from all sources, including cosmic rays, X-rays, television sets and atmospheric nuclear tests accumulates to about 100–150 millirem per year, and one transatlantic crossing in a subsonic or supersonic transport adds 3 millirem to that total. There are greater dangers to be found from crossing the road than from this. Suggestions that Concorde should only be staffed by stewardesses beyond child bearing age, just turned out to be stories designed to attract popular press headlines.

As far as the pollution of the atmosphere is concerned only hydrogen-fuelled engines are completely 'clean' – that is if the water vapour they emit is ignored. Fossil-fuelled engines also emit water vapour. Often the critics could not make up their minds whether the presence of extra water vapour would 'cut off the sun's rays from the ground and bring on a new ice age', or 'give rise to a "hot house" effect and overheat the earth'. In practice the earth's weather systems are infinitely more responsible for the distribution of water vapour than aircraft can ever be. As for other pollutants, cars are nearly ten times worse per seat mile than Concorde, and there are many cars.

Of the most serious concern to the critics was the noise that they believed Concorde would cause at airports. For efficiency at supersonic speeds SSTs then had to be fitted with engines which have a high velocity jet efflux. The shearing effect of this efflux with the static air to the rear of an aircraft causes the major part of the noise. Consistent with retaining an efficient engine, Concorde's manufacturers had gone to enormous lengths to reduce engine noise. They had concentrated on two areas. One was to break down the sharp boundary between the moving and static air and the other was to try and increase the quantity of air flowing through the engine so that it would give the same thrust with a lower exhaust velocity.

The first line of attack saw the development of a device called 'spades'. These were designed to break up the efflux by protruding rectangular metal plates into the jet pipe to splay out the jet efflux during take-off, to

be retracted when engine silencing was not required. The 'spades' appeared quite promising in miniature, but failed to be sufficiently effective on the full-scale engine, and were abandoned. Another device called 'buckets' was more successful. Consisting of a pair of doors rather like eyelids, they are set to the rear of the jet pipe of each engine, being visible from the outside of the aircraft. During flight at low speed they mix the static and engine exhaust air thus breaking up the noisy boundary. On landing they are used as thrust reversers by closing off the jet pipe and deflecting the efflux forward; in supersonic flight they form a divergent exit nozzle (see photograph on page 22).

The second line of attack on the noise front involved computer control of the relative speeds of two engine shafts allowing the engine to 'change gear'. This happens after Concorde takes-off and allows a greater mass of air into the engine, thus causing the velocity of the jet efflux to be reduced without the loss of thrust. Such a process can only be applied after Concorde has sufficient forward speed for the intakes to swallow enough air; insufficient air could lead to a surge (backfire).

Whatever the manufacturers achieved in

Concorde 002 on take-off. The 'production' Olympus engine has a modified combustion chamber which eliminates these smoky emissions. Also changed were the auxiliary inlet doors from the 'scoop' (shown here), to the 'blow-in' type. The variable 'ramps' are visible in the intake entrances. The failure and throwing forward of one of these from number 4 intake and its ingestion by the number 3 engine during a test flight at Mach 2 on 001, caused a double engine failure. The subsequent safe return to base proved the soundness of Concorde's basic design, in contrast to the Hustler (see page 40)

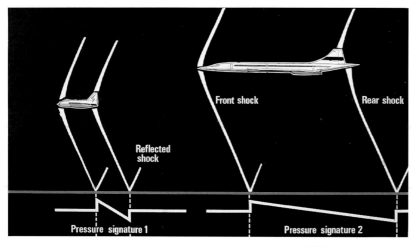

The pressure signatures from supersonic aircraft of different lengths.
Note this diagram does not show the refraction of the shock waves
due to increasing temperature and changing winds as they approach
the earth's surface

Pressure Waves at less than
Mach 1.0

Pressure Waves at Mach 1.0

Envelope of Pressure Waves
'Shock Wave' above Mach 1.0

the way of noise reduction, the crews having
reduced to minimum thrust consistent with
climbing, to comply with noise abatement
procedures had to eke out every last ounce
of the aircraft's performance. However, such
procedures had not been finally and
accurately formulated for use during the
route proving flights flown by Concorde
during the summer of 1975. Concorde was
thus rather noisier than she should have
been, with the result that the American anti-
Concorde lobby found some rather willing
allies in Britain.

The worst aspect of the anti-Concorde
campaign was the way in which the critics
were quite happy to see Concorde written
off before being allowed into New York
without a fair noise trial. There was much
discussion in the media about this but
eventually, when services began, the combination of the relatively light take-off
weights (less fuel is required on a New York
to London sector than vice versa) and the
meticulous application of the noise abatement procedures kept Concorde's noise well
within limits. The protestors melted away.
Since then Concorde has made many firm
friends with the people in New York.

Nevertheless a second generation SST
will have to be quieter than Concorde.
Several fully laden Concorde departures per
day can be tolerated by most people but one
every ten minutes from the more land locked
airfields could be problematic.

The noise
monitoring posts at
Kennedy. The two
most desirable
runways for
Concorde on take-off
are 31L and 22R. By
turning away from
the noise sensitive
areas after take-off,
most of the noise
impact of Concorde
at Kennedy was
avoided. Runways 4L,
4R and 13L are never
used by Concorde at
transatlantic take-off
weights

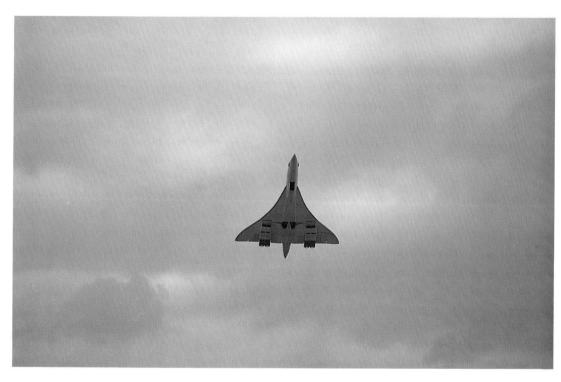

Opposite
The build up of the shock waves. As the aircraft approaches the speed of sound, the molecules of air progressively have less 'warning' of the approach of the aircraft. Above Mach 1 a shock wave forms, tangential to the spheres of disturbance. Some Concorde critics appeared to think that Concorde formed a shock wave at any speed. Under normal conditions, due to its refraction in the warmer atmosphere beneath the aircraft, the shock wave from Concorde only reaches the ground when Concorde exceeds Mach 1.15. The shock wave first -reaches the ground about 50 miles after the 'acceleration point'

In January 1976 the final battle for entry to New York still lay in the future. British Airways and Air France were patiently putting the finishing touches to a plan for a joint take-off into the supersonic era; the British with a Concorde from Heathrow and the French with a Concorde from Charles de Gaulle.

On 21 January 1976 I stood with my wife, camera at the ready at the take-off end of runway 28 left at London's Heathrow airport. Around us were crowds of people, some were wearing heavy looking 'service' earphones connected to electronic devices wired up to microphones on poles. Concorde would not start her commercial supersonic service unrecorded! We listened to a local radio broadcast. At 11.40 precisely the commentator announced that Concorde had begun to roll. Next came the distinctive sound of the four reheated Olympus engines. Then Concorde GBOAA came in view, climbing out over the approach lights

*Airlife, 1984

This publicity photograph, inset, was taken on Concorde G-BBDG (202) as can be seen from the instrumentation on the engineers' panel which was different from that ultimately fitted to the production Concordes

The most extensive test programme ever undertaken for a commercial airliner (5500 hours of which 2000 were supersonic) included cold weather trials – Concorde 02 at Fairbanks, Alaska (Latitude 65N)

Opposite page In contrast to her difficulties in 1976 and 1977 Concorde has become a welcome visitor to many US destinations. In November 1984 Concorde GBOAB visited Boeing Field at Seattle, Washington State. Mount Rainier can be seen in the background. For the visit the Boeing Museum of Flight displayed a model of the cancelled US SST project, the B2707-200; they also organised a supersonic flight by Concorde out over the Pacific and back for one hundred passengers to raise funds for the museum

of the reciprocal runway, with the undercarriage retracting. Commercial supersonic services had begun.

As the British Concorde, under the command of Captain Norman Todd, with Captain Brian Calvert as second-in-command and Senior Engineer Officer John Lidiard, reached her subsonic cruising altitude over the English Channel, the crew heard that the Air France Concorde F-BVFA had had an equally successful departure. The odds, people had said, were heavily against achieving a simultaneous take-off, but as so often in the past Concorde had proved the pessimists wrong.

Concorde F-BVFA flew to Rio de Janeiro via Dakar; G-BOAA flew to Bahrain. Included amongst the guests on G-BOAA were Sir George Edwards (Chairman of BAC) and Sir Stanley Hooker. On arrival at Bahrain they were invited to a banquet at the New Palace by the Amir of Bahrain. Sir Stanley Hooker, in his book *Not Much of an Engineer,** said: 'Eventually we entered the fabulous dining room, ritually washed our hands and took our places around the gigantic U-shaped table. I was next to the Minister of Foreign Trade, who spoke perfect English. We each had a waiter in full court uniform, each pair of guests being supervised by a steward . . . I was about to turn to the Minister and say "How far sighted and generous of your government to allow us to bring the Concorde here on its first scheduled flight" when he said to me "what a great honour you have done our country by bringing your magnificent Concorde here on its inaugural flight!" Considering the violent hullabaloo that was going on in New York, and that nobody else would allow us in, it was difficult to find the right answer!'

Left to right Senior Engineer Officer John Lidiard, Captain Norman Todd and Captain Brian Calvert – the crew of the inaugural service to Bahrain on 21 January 1976 on Concorde G-BOAA.

The Turn of the Tide

During the early days of supersonic services to Bahrain in 1976, Concorde was hardly ever out of the headlines. 'US warned against ban on Concorde'; 'Court challenge on Concorde go-ahead'; 'Red light delays Concorde'; 'Boeing tries for rival to Concorde.' Under this headline from *The Times* (3 April 1976) Mr Lloyd Goodmanson, Boeing's design director said '... much of the official opposition to giving British Airways and Air France landing rights for Concorde was based on pure jealousy of their commercial lead rather than environmental considerations.'

Concorde had many vociferous friends and enemies. But for Concorde to succeed she needed landing rights in the United States, and at New York in particular.

Two production lines for Concorde had been set up at vast expense, one in Toulouse, France, and the other at Filton, in Britain.

Apart from the availability and skills of a work force, production lines require the necessary jigs and tools, but above all factory space. In 1974 the Governments of Britain and France had approved the building of 16 production Concordes. This was in spite of Pan American and TWA having decided in 1973 not to take up their options on buying Concorde. It was hoped that now Concorde had started services, these airlines might change their minds.

Iran Air and China Airlines had also shown an interest in Concorde, but they, in line with the rest of the world's airlines, were keeping very quiet on the subject. Production lines cannot remain open indefinitely while aircraft cannot go on being produced without prospective customers, and Concorde production facilities would have to make way for other work. By 1976 it was deemed that it was up to Air France and

Meeting at Dulles tower. Scheduled Concorde services to Washington's Dulles airport began on 24 May 1976

Opposite page A slender delta pivots around the slender CN tower. Concorde is a frequent visitor to the Toronto Airshow in Canada

I FOUND THIS PART TIME JOB UNTIL NEW YORK MAKES UP ITS MIND

PAIGE

From The Times, *Friday 19 August 1977*

British Airways to make a success of the new supersonic era. However, without permission to fly to the USA, this appeared almost impossible.

On 4 February 1976, after protracted wrangling, the US Secretary of Transportation, William T. Coleman, finally gave approval for British Airways and Air France to commence services for a 16 month trial period; one Concorde each per day to Washington and two each per day to New York. On 24 May 1976 Concorde services began to Dulles airport at Washington, owned by the Federal (US Government) authorities. In the words of Brian Calvert, Commander of that first flight: 'Planning started for what, it was decided, would be another spectacular – this time a joint arrival. We agreed that on this occasion the British Airways flight would land first – simultaneous landings were a little too much to expect.' The two Concordes performed perfectly, as they had done almost exactly four months earlier at the start of their commercial careers.

Landing Concorde at Dulles International airport Washington, was one thing, but permission to do so at Kennedy airport, New York, owned by the Port of New York Authority, was another. Coleman had implied that Federal pressure might be brought to bear on the Authority, but it became increasingly apparent that there would have to be a legal battle before Concorde could gain rights into New York.

Those rights were finally granted, and amidst threats of the greatest car-borne anti-SST demonstration, Concorde 201 (F-WTSB) arrived in New York on 19 October 1977. In command was Aerospatiale's Chief Test Pilot, Jean Franchi and on the flight deck with him were Captain Brian Walpole (BA Flight Technical Manager) and Captain Pierre Dudal of Air France. The following day with Captain Walpole in command, Concorde took off from runway 31L (the left hand of the two north-westerly facing runways at New York). For the first time Concorde made the famous left hand climbing turn, started at 100 ft above the runway. That turn, which was regarded as cheating the noise meters by some critics, had been the subject of much practice, both at other airfields and in the Concorde simulators. The turn, the maintenance of the correct speeds, the cutting back of the thrust, the re-application, the cutting back and finally the re-application of thrust had been calculated precisely to correspond with Concorde's proximity to noise sensitive areas. The take-off was a success, the noise minimal. In one sense the protestors had won a great victory: Concorde had been made to be acceptably quiet and other airliners had better follow Concorde's example. On 22 November 1977 British Airways and Air France commenced supersonic services to New York.

Had there been no delay in starting the New York service, there might have been further orders for Concorde. But however 'well dressed' Concorde had appeared, no purchasers were forthcoming while she had 'nowhere to go.'

In December 1977 British Airways, in conjunction with Singapore Airlines (SIA), extended the London to Bahrain Concorde service to Singapore. During performance and hot weather trials in September 1974 the first 'production' Concorde (GBBDG), with Brian Trubshaw and Peter Baker (Assistant Chief test pilot BAC) at the controls, had flown supersonically over India. Supersonic overflying permission was now withdrawn so the Concorde route to Singapore had to go to the south of Sri Lanka adding some 200 nautical miles (10 minutes flying time). By December 1977 minor modifications and improved operating procedures had increased Concorde's range, so, what would have been unattainable in early 1976, was by then quite possible. However, after three return flights the Malaysian government withdrew flying rights over the Straits of Malacca. After more negotiations with the Malaysians the route reopened in January 1979 and was operated until November 1980. Concorde was flown to Singapore by BA crews with the cabin alternatively being staffed by BA and Singapore Airlines cabin crews.

World recession brought about a drop in

Concorde's load figures between London and Singapore. This, coupled with the financial arrangements between British Airways and Singapore Airlines, put a greater share of the burden of loss onto British Airways, finally causing the route to be abandoned. A particular Concorde had been earmarked for use on this route (G-BOAD), being painted in Singapore livery on the left hand side, and in BA colours on the right. This was the first and, by 1990, the only Concorde to have appeared in colours of an airline other than those of Air France or British Airways. Sadly, as the route closed down, the BA flight deck crews returned home from their postings in Singapore. With an excess of crews, some would leave and others be redeployed in the airline. Morale which was usually very high, took a temporary dip. G-BOAD was restored to BA livery.

Earlier that same year the agreement between Air France, British Airways and Braniff which enabled Concorde to continue through to Dallas, Texas, from Washington (changing to an all American crew just for this sector), was wound up. The route lasted from January 1979 until June 1980. Braniff was, by 1990, the only American airline to have operated Concorde, albeit subsonically. They had hoped to gain experience with the aircraft for eventual supersonic services to South American destinations. In the meantime Concorde's high profile would have helped their marketing effort. But world recession and the deregulation of American internal airline routes had stretched Braniff's resources, so their Concorde operation experienced unacceptably low loads. On the Washington to Dallas sector the Concordes bore their home airlines' livery, the only noticeable external change being the dropping of the 'G' in the registration which in the case of the British Concorde had been changed from the usual British registration of a 'G' followed by four letters, to a 'G' followed by an 'N' two single digit numbers and the two final letters of the original British registration.

To give Concorde a boost during the time when services were declining, several Concorde crew members chartered the aircraft, giving people flights on Concorde at a fraction of the cost of a transatlantic fare. The first one to do so was a Concorde stewardess, Jeannette Hartley, who organised charters, at no little financial risk to herself. In 1981 my wife and I chartered Concorde to celebrate Britain winning the Schneider Trophy contest. The last contest was won in 1931 by an RAF team captained by Squadron Leader A. H. Orlebar*. In 1981 Concorde flew on two occasions, at 340 mph, almost exactly 1000 mph less than her cruising speed, around the final course which was situated between the Isle of Wight and Portsmouth (England). The speed of 340 mph was chosen since it had

Overleaf *G-BOAD showing Singapore Airlines colours on the port (left) side, taking off from Heathrow for the nine hour journey to Singapore*

*A cousin of the Author.

NEW YORK POST, THURSDAY, MAY 12, 1977

"Damn the court, DON'T LET IT LAND!!"

Opposite, below
*Concorde G-BOAA
with the Anglo
American registration
G-N94AA during the
period when Braniff
operated Concordes
between Washington
Dulles and Dallas
Fort Worth. Note the
curves on the leading
edge of the wing,
necessary for the
smooth transition
from lift generated by
vortices, roughly
below 250 knots, to
lift from a
'conventional'
attached airflow,
generated at the
higher speeds*

*Concorde was
chartered on 12 and
13 September, 1981,
by the author to
mark this event. Each
of the passengers
received a certificate
like this one. The
Captain on those
occasions was John
Eames, the author
was First Officer and
Senior Engineer
Officer David
Macdonald, the Flight
Engineer*

been the average speed of Flt. Lt. John Boothman's winning Supermarine S6B in 1931. Two Schneider trophy pilots flew on Concorde to celebrate the 50th Anniversary of the final victory: Air Commodore D'Arcy Greig (1929 team) and Group Captain Leonard Snaith (1931 team).

Other Concorde crew members followed suit.

On Concorde's financial side, a review in February 1979 of the ability of British Airways to make a profit with Concorde had concluded that it could not do so by ordinary commercial standards. Accordingly the Labour Government decided to write off the £160m of Public Dividend Capital (PDC) associated with BA's acquisition of its five Concordes. In November 1979 an Industry and Trade Select Committee, chaired by Sir Donald Kaberry MP, was convened. This was to investigate Concorde. Quoting from the report of their investigations (published in 1981): '... this [the writing off of £160m PDC] meant that the whole fleet, including the initial inventory of spares, was entered in the British Airways balance sheet as a fully depreciated asset – that is to say a gift from the taxpayer. For their part British Airways had to pay to the Government 80 per cent of future Concorde operating surpluses (the so called 80:20 agreement), though these were to be calculated after the offset of any operating deficits incurred after the review and also the amortised cost of any post-review expenditure.'

The BA partnership deal with Singapore Airlines (SIA) on the Singapore route negotiated by Gordon Davidson (Concorde Marketing Director, BA 1975–1979), appeared promising for BA, but it had dashed

Government hopes of SIA purchasing at least one of the remaining unsold Concordes – two in Britain and three in France. Later the best return for the Government appeared to come from placing the two unsold

SCHNEIDER TROPHY
50th Anniversary Flight by
British airways **Concorde**

1931   1981

British

Presented to

_____

who flew in Concorde to mark the event
on 13th September 1981

Christopher J. Orlebar

British Concordes with British airlines. When Gordon Davidson moved to British Caledonian, rumours started of BCal operating a supersonic service to Lagos, but this came to nothing. For a period BA operated one of the two surplus Concordes when one of its Concordes was undergoing modifications. Ultimately BA acquired the two remaining Concordes, making seven in all.

According to the Report, the UK had

spent about £900 million on Concorde by the end of 1980. Furthermore the Government was still having to finance the support given by the manufacturers to the project, expected to total £123 million for the five years beginning 1980/81.

During the commercial life of an aircraft, its manufacturers not only undertake to supply spare parts, but just as importantly to supply a 'support' service in the form of carrying out development work and monitoring performance, suggesting or insisting, where necessary, on improvements or modifications. Overseeing this process are the aviation authorities in whose countries the aircraft are built and registered – the CAA (Civil Aviation Authority) in Britain. These aviation authorities have the full backing of their country's law behind them. Such support is usually financed from profits from the sale of spare parts to the airlines.

In the case of Concorde, monitoring of the aircraft's performance was, in the early days of operation, a very expensive business. Not least of those expenses were the two test specimens – full-sized Concorde fuselages dedicated to being tested on the ground. Quite early in the programme the stress test specimen in France had been purposely tested to destruction, but the one at Farnborough, was still by 1980 costing several millions per year to run. This Concorde had been dedicated to being 'flight cycled', which included the heating and cooling process experienced on every supersonic sector. Profits through sales of spare parts would not raise anything like enough to pay for the Farnborough rig, nor enough to pay for the necessary, but diminishing, development work associated with Concorde. Accordingly, the four manufacturers – Aerospatiale, British Aerospace (successors to BAC), Rolls-Royce and SNECMA – were funded for their responsibilities to Concorde by their respective governments.

In October 1978 the jigs used to manufacture Concorde were removed from the Brabazon Hangers at Filton for storage at Wroughton, near Swindon in Wiltshire, against the possibility that there might be a demand for more Concordes. However, the French had, by December 1977, not only removed but disposed of their jigs; with their capability gone further production of Concordes would have been an extra expense. On 31 December 1980 it was announced that the production phase of Concorde had ended, but it was not until

The Stress Fatigue Specimen at CEAT (Centre d'Essais Aeronautique de Toulouse), one of the two complete Concorde airframes dedicated to structural tests. This specimen was not subjected to heating and cooling to simulate a supersonic flight cycle, as was the one at Farnborough

Inlet
Upper Wing

Inlet
Fuselage & Fin

Inlet
Lower Wing

**Concorde Major Fatigue Test
Thermal Duct**

October 1981 that disposal to scrap merchants of the stored British jigs began. About this time Federal Express investigated the use of Concorde as a supersonic parcel carrier, but this also came to nothing.

The Select Committee, charged to look into Concorde affairs, had to face some rather unpalatable truths. No more Concordes would be sold, the funding of the manufacturers would bring no return to the Governments, and the two airlines concerned did not seem able to operate Concorde profitably. It had been asked to make recommendations specifically on the question of costs due to be met out of the public purse. Was there, it tried to answer, a case for continued expenditure, which although unjustifiable in financial terms, might confer other benefits on the UK, such as prestige or the basis for starting a second generation SST? Then, more sinisterly, from Concorde's point of view, the Committee was to investigate how the cost of immediate cancellation would compare with the cost of continuing and how a proposal to cancel would affect relations between the UK and France.

The Committee heard evidence from representatives of British Airways, the British manufacturers of Concorde (British Aerospace and Rolls-Royce), the Minister of Trade and Industry (Norman Tebbit, an ex BOAC pilot), and the Deputy and Assistant Secretaries of the Department of Industry. Representing Concorde's paymasters, the Select Committee had every right to question the commercial decisions made by the companies responsible for servicing and operating Concorde.

It appeared that the writing was on the wall for Concorde, the more so since the return of a Conservative Government in May 1979. There is no doubt that they wished Concorde to continue if at all possible, but not at any price.

The change of government in Britain also saw a change of policy towards the nationalized industries. In February 1981, Ross Stainton retired as Chairman of the British Airways Board, and Sir John King took over. He had been charged by the Government to prepare the company for privatisation. Having suffered disappointing financial results, attributable to the world recession, the moment had arrived to study every aspect of the airline with the view to cutting costs and increasing revenue. Nevertheless, the new leadership was more keen than the old on retaining Concorde.

All too frequently large organisations become conscious that their staff can lose a sense of identity and pride in their work. Following the period of recession, the restoration of morale in British Airways was regarded as a most important part in its march back to profitability. To this end, 'profit centres' were set up within the airline. One such centre was the Concorde Division. In May 1982, Captain Brian Walpole, who had been Flight Manager Technical was

Opposite, top The Concorde Fatigue Specimen at the Royal Aircraft Establishment (RAE), Farnborough. Although fully visible, here the airframe was festooned with ducts connected to a hot air supply in order to simulate the heating and cooling experienced by a Concorde on a supersonic flight. Each 'flight' was minutely monitored by computers. With sufficient experience to allow Concordes to fly well into the 21st century, this specimen was dismantled in 1985

Opposite, below The Concorde Fatigue Specimen engulfed by its thermal duct. The thinness of the wing tips and top of the fin meant that they would not suffer significant thermal fatigue, hence they were not under test. The fuel tanks were filled, the cabin pressurised and jacks were used to 'load' the airframe as on a real flight

The BA 195 being prepared for service at Heathrow on a winter's evening. Later, from the west, the sun will rise on this Concorde for the second time in the day. For a while during the early 1980s the livery excluded the word 'Airways'

FIRST CONCORDE TO PITTSBURGH!
BRITISH AIRWAYS – 11 MAY 1985

Concorde is frequently chartered to destinations all over America. On this occasion, two weeks after the unveiling of the new livery, Concorde was used to publicise the opening of the Jumbo service between London and Pittsburgh via Washington

Opposite, top Washington Dulles, September 1985, passengers disembarking from G-BOAA via the 'Mobile Lounge'. Once loaded the lounge is lowered prior to driving to the terminal building. After a 50 minute turn round the aircraft will be en route to Miami

Centre Concorde G-BOAA inaugural service to Miami from London via Washington, 27 March 1984. The 1 hour 20 minute sector from Washington to Miami is flown at subsonic speeds over land then at supersonic speeds over the sea south of Wilmington, North Carolina

asked by Gerry Draper (BA Commercial Director) to become General Manager of this new division. As his assistant he brought with him another Concorde pilot, Senior First Officer W. D. (Jock) Lowe. Broadly they divided their responsibilities into two, Walpole looking into ways of increasing revenue and Lowe at ways of reducing costs. The appointment of practising pilots to these positions represented a welcome change from tradition. However, it must be stated that their predecessors in Commercial Division had worked very hard for Concorde's success in conditions which had not been easy. At that time Concorde passenger loads were falling from their peak in 1979 while costs consistently exceeded revenue.

Within months of their new appointment Concorde was faced by a new crisis. In August 1982 Ian Sproat (MP) wrote to Sir John King stating the Government's intention to cease funding the British manufacturers support costs for Concorde and asking British Airways if it wished to take on this responsibility. If BA were to decline, in the words of Keith Wilkins (Head of Planning, BA): 'The supersonic project would terminate.' Termination in Britain at this stage would probably have meant termination in France as well. The date set for this was 31 March 1983.

President Mitterand, unlike his predecessor, did countenance a review of Concorde's financial performance when he came to power in 1980 and Concorde was on the agenda of the Anglo-French summit of 1981. However, at no time in Concorde's history had Britain and France both shared the same opinion regarding cancellation, hence its survival. In Britain at this time, the

Government perceived that by 1983 or 1984 the 80:20 agreement might even be producing a return from which the support costs could be financed, especially since the cancellation of the Singapore route. But Government involvement of this kind was not within the philosophy of the Conservative party in power. Probably for this reason, rather than from wishing to stop Concorde, did Ian Sproat write to Sir John King stating the Government's intention of ceasing to fund the British manufacturers.

*See page 73.

An Air France Concorde being prepared for service at Kennedy in October, 1985. By 1984 Air France Concorde operations became profitable on the Paris New York route. Runway 22R is one of those preferred for a Concorde take-off on the basis of restricting noise (see page 60). There are no similar restrictions for Concordes landing at Kennedy

The BA reply indicated that they were very willing to examine the possibility of taking over the support costs, but they would have to be given time to examine the implications. The Government agreed to another year being made available before the axe would finally fall on public money funding the British manufacturers. In the meantime a Department of Trade and Industry Review Group headed by Mr Bruce MacTavish of the Civil Service, would negotiate with BA for the handing over of the Government's responsibility to BA. The BA negotiating team were led by Mr Keith Wilkins (Head of Planning), with Captain Walpole (General Manager Concorde Division), Jock Lowe (Planning Manager Concorde), Sandy Sell (Engineering), and Peter Brass (Accounting).

The team's first job was to find out whether Concorde could make a sufficient operating surplus to fund the British manufacturers' support costs. Their second, and no less important, task was to analyse the manufacturers' activities with a view to reducing costs without impairing service, especially in areas of flight safety. This would rule out any development work not called for jointly by manufacturers and BA. The team were modestly optimistic that Concorde revenue which, had, in the period 1979/80 to 1982/83 been dropping, would improve as the recession passed. Over optimism was not only unwarranted, but might have upset the negotiations. Equally too much pessimism might have brought the negotiations to an untimely end. It took eighteen months to find a satisfactory formula.

The main points at issue were the terms surrounding the acquisition by BA of Concorde spare parts owned by the Government (and useless to anyone other than a Concorde operator), the winding up of the 80:20 agreement soon expected to give government a small dividend, and the replacement of the Government by BA in the contracts with the British manufacturers (British Aerospace and Rolls-Royce). On this particular issue it was fundamental that BA could withdraw unilaterally from the Concorde project at its own discretion without having to finance the British manufacturers if Air France continued Concorde operations. BA made it clear to the Government that they would not pay for the continuation of the operation of the test rig at Farnborough. This had been a major element in the support costs and by 1984 the

full-scale Concorde structure had experienced sufficient 'flight cycles' for the Concordes to continue, at their present rate of use, well into the next century*. In the end BA took responsibility for the dismantling of the rig.

The funding of Concorde's French manufacturers would not necessarily be altered by the proposed changes in Britain – that was a French matter. Hitherto the French manufacturers had received payment from the French Government. In the early 1980s the French Government had promised Air France that it would bear a higher proportion of its Concorde operating loss. In return it reserved the right to dictate where Air France operated Concorde. With the result that the Rio de Janeiro, Caracas and Mexico through Washington routes were abandoned leaving Air France a single daily return Concorde service between Paris and New York. In 1984 Air France operations became profitable.

In April 1983, as discussions between BA and the Government continued, a 30 minute documentary programme about Concorde appeared in the QED series of BBC1. I was technical consultant to the producer, Brian Johnson, and was present as First Officer to Brian Walpole on the London to New York service which was filmed. (The Flight Engineer on that sector was Senior Engineer Officer Bill Johnstone.) Brian Walpole, during an interview on the programme, made it very clear that Concorde in future would have to stand on its own two feet: 'I believe it can, and, given a reasonable response from Government, Concorde will continue.' Although the tide had started to turn in favour of Concorde before the transmission of that programme, it was from that moment that Concorde ceased to be regarded as a loss maker. Gone were the tiresome yet familiar gibes about its poor prospects.

Slowly and inexorably the negotiations eroded the major outstanding differences between the Government and BA. In the end a sum had to be agreed which BA would pay to the Government for all the Concorde spares, Concorde G-BBDG (202) which was grounded at Filton minus engines and much equipment, the Farnborough Concorde test structure, as well as buying its way out of the 80:20 agreement. In March 1984, eighteen months of detailed analysis were brought to a swift conclusion. In a meeting lasting not more than a quarter of an hour, reminiscent of bargaining in an eastern bazaar, Gordon Dunlop (Finance Director of BA) and the Government representatives agreed on a figure: £16.5m. Concorde was saved.

Great credit is due to the people whose determination found a way of preserving this unique aircraft in service. In particular, Bruce MacTavish as negotiator for the Government and Keith Wilkins astute leader of the BA team deserve great praise. Brian Walpole's and Jock Lowe's infectious enthusiasm and dedication to Concorde were great motivators throughout. During all the negotiations Concorde continued in service thanks to everyone connected with the operation maintaining faith that somehow Concorde would have a successful future.

A Conservative Government spawned Concorde and ensured its right to life through an unbreakable treaty with France in 1962. Twenty-one years (and a few months) later, another Conservative Government severed almost all its financial connections with Concorde; the supersonic airliner had come of age. With expanding charter services and improving figures on the scheduled routes (London to New York and London to Washington and Miami), the commercial future of Concorde in British Airways looked bright.

Top
Maintenance at Heathrow, and here Concorde is festooned with gantries designed for ease of access

Above
The 9½ ft diameter cabin without seats. The outside rails on which the seats are fixed are mounted so that they are not stretched due to the elongation of the fuselage which is at 100°C during cruise, compared to the 22°C of the cabin

Right
The walkway around the nose, here at 12½° down, is contoured to fit precisely. The gap in the nose is open for access to the weather radar scanner. Note the windscreen wipers revealed with the visor down

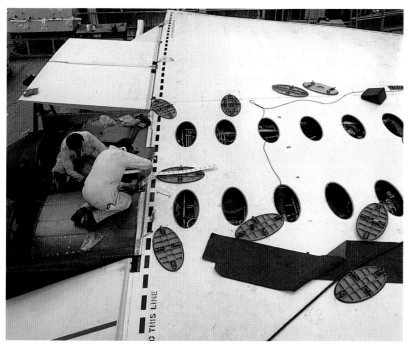

Above left
One of the hydraulic jacks responsible for moving the elevons. Normally it is signalled electrically; although there is an 'emergency' mechanical signalling system, there is no 'manual reversion'. Should hydraulic pressure from the engine pumps fail, a slip-stream driven hydraulic air turbine can be deployed to supply pressure, seen here ahead of the jack

Middle left
Concorde inspires great dedication and enthusiasm among all those whose privilege it is to contribute to the supersonic operation, not least from the maintenance engineers, the unsung heroes of the Concorde Story

Above
One of the eight fan-cooled 'carbon' brake units on Concorde. The development of carbon fibre instead of steel represented a great weight saving. Thanks to Concorde such brakes have become common place on subsonic airliners

Below left
A view forward from the tail fin during maintenance

The Flight – Acceleration

The flight deck. The two control columns with their familiar 'ramshorns' shape can be seen. To the right is the Flight Engineer's panel. The nose and visor were down when this picture was taken during a period of servicing in the hangar. Unpowered, the instruments display red failure flags

'Ladies and gentlemen. This is the First Officer, Christopher Orlebar,' comes the voice on the cabin address system. 'We are climbing through 20,000 ft and are just accelerating through the cruising speed of a Jumbo jet: Mach 0.85, 550 miles per hour. We are flying over the track of Brunel's Great Western Railway – another great engineering project – towards Bristol, and in particular Filton, from where this Concorde first flew in 1979.

'The time in New York, if you would like to reset your watches is five minutes to six. We expect to arrive in New York at a quarter past nine. Having left London at ten thirty, you do not need to be an Einsteinean physicist to work out that that will make us one and a quarter hours younger by the time we arrive at Kennedy airport. Although we travel backwards in time it is not sufficiently far to call our destination by any of its original names – Idlewild, or New Amsterdam.

'In six minutes from now we shall be switching on the after-burners. You will feel two small nudges as they come on in pairs. They give extra thrust to the engines to overcome the increased air resistance found during supersonic flight. We accelerate and climb, and by 43,500 ft we shall have achieved Mach 1.7, at which point the after-burners will be switched off. In case there are no thermodynamicists among you I will explain why. By Mach 1.7 the engines will have become very much more efficient due to the increase in airflow through the intakes, which precompress and slows down the air before it enters the engines. There is then sufficient thrust to overcome the increased air resistance caused by those shock waves which appeared just below Mach 1. We continue to climb and accelerate, reaching Mach 2 just above 50,000 ft. Thereafter we climb gently as we use the fuel and so become lighter, maintaining Mach 2, or thereabouts, until we reach today's ceiling of about 58,000 ft – in any case not above 60,000 ft which is as high as we are allowed to fly.'

Another voice now, this time in the headsets of the crew, from the Air Traffic Controller at West Drayton: 'Speedbird Concorde one nine three*, London. You are cleared to climb at the acceleration point. Cross eight degrees west at or above flight level four three zero (43,000 ft).'

'Roger. Cleared to climb at the accele-

system, which allows landings in visibilities down to 200 metres (656 ft) with a 'decision height' (whether to land or to go up again) of 15 ft (4.5 metres). Whatever the weather at the destination, the aircraft must be able to divert to an alternate airfield whose weather would allow an ordinary manual landing. The weather at the en-route alternate airfields is also checked. These might be needed in the event of engine failure when Concorde would be forced to decelerate to

*In 1987 the flight number of BA 193 was changed to BA 001.

Senior Flight Engineer Tony Brown (left), Captain John Massie (centre), and the author at the flight briefing in the Queen's Building at Heathrow

ration point. Cross eight degrees west flight level four three zero or above. Speedbird Concorde one nine three,' comes the reply to London Air Traffic Control. Soon Concorde will be travelling at almost two and a half times the speed of a Jumbo jet.

Two hours previously the three flight deck crew of BA 193* assembled in the Queen's building at London's Heathrow Airport.

'One hundred [passengers] booked. You have Alpha Foxtrot on stand Juliet 2.' Armed with this information and a list of the six cabin crew members, the three crew, consisting of Captain, First Officer and Flight Engineer, go to be briefed. They study the weather, the fuel flight plan and other relevant information concerning airfields, navigation aids and route information.

The weather forecast at the destination and alternate airfields is of fundamental significance. Is fog likely? Concorde is fitted with a Category Three automatic landing

Air temperature gauge on Concorde at Mach 2. The outside air temperature is shown in the 'static' box. The tip of the nose in the 'Total' box and the deviation from the International Standard Atmosphere in the 'ISA' box

subsonic speeds where the range is not so great.

The forecast winds between 50,000 ft and 60,000 ft are studied. They are usually less strong than the winds found up to 40,000 ft. Very rarely do they exceed 100 knots. On average they blow from the west at 30 knots. Cruising at 1,150 knots true airspeed, a 100 knot headwind has less effect on Concorde than on a Jumbo which cruises at 480 knots. Over a 2,000 nautical mile (nm) distance a 100 knot headwind gives Concorde a ground speed of 1,050 knots increasing the flight time by 10 minutes, but a Jumbo with a ground speed of 380 knots would take 65 minutes longer over the same distance. The tracks followed by subsonic aircraft over the Atlantic are varied from day to day to take account of the winds. The supersonic tracks, however, are fixed by the minimum distance consistent with over-water flight where the sonic boom is acceptable.

The temperature to be found at altitude is also of importance. The average over the Atlantic constantly varies, but is of the order of minus 55°C (−67°F) at Concorde's cruising level. A few degrees warmer and the fuel requirement is greater and vice versa. For efficiency the engines prefer cold air. There is a greater mass of oxygen in a given volume of air at a given pressure, in cold air than in hot air.

The fuel required to carry 10 tonnes of payload (100 passengers and their luggage) and 15 tonnes of spare fuel over the 3,150 nm between London and New York is typically 77 tonnes (depending on winds and temperatures). Nevertheless the fuel flight plan is meticulously checked. For taxiing at London 1.4 tonnes are added bringing the total to 93.4 tonnes – some 2 tonnes short of full tanks. The expected take-off weight with these figures is 180 tonnes. The expected flight time on this journey is 3 hours and 23 minutes.

Equipped with the paperwork the crew are driven to the aircraft on stand Juliet 2. At this stage the gleaming paintwork showing off the new British Airways Concorde livery (unveiled 25 April 1985) is somewhat hidden by hordes of service vehicles, fuel bowsers, luggage and catering trucks and transport vans. The passengers congregating in the special Concorde lounge glimpse the unique supersonic nose serene above the white-overalled activity beneath.

It is almost impossible for the passenger, viewing all this activity, to imagine just how many lifetimes of thought and effort

preceded this moment of sublime anticipation: flying the world's only successful supersonic airliner. Yet as these words are written, powered flight by men in heavier than air machines has happened well within the lifespan of many living people and commercial supersonic flight is 10 years old.

The 'safety' checks having been completed in the cockpit, the pilots remain on board while the Flight Engineer checks the exterior of the aircraft. He will inspect, amongst other things, landing gear, tyres, engine intakes and the elevons (the flying control surfaces) to the rear of the wing, which look, without hydraulic pressure, rather like flaps in the 'down' position. As he does so he steps over power cables, refuelling hoses and the high-pressure air hoses for use during engine starting. Finally he rejoins the pilots going through their 'scan' checks. Lights, instruments and audio warnings are all scrutinised. 'Pull up, pull up!' says an insistent microchip from the loudspeakers. It is the terrain avoidance system under test. Another voice, taped and transmitted from the tower, announces: 'This is Heathrow information Romeo, zero eight one five weather, wind two nine zero degrees, one five knots ...' The data is copied down, relevant for calculating whether conditions are suitable to allow 180 tonnes of Concorde to take-off from runway 28 left (the southerly of the two west facing runways at Heathrow).

Although more crowded with instruments than other airliners, the cockpit in Concorde is equipped with the familiar ones: altimeters, airspeed indicators, artificial horizons and engine temperature and pressure instruments. However, the Mach-meters are calibrated up to Mach 2.4, and on closer inspection switches and gauges of systems unique to Concorde become apparent – engine air intake controls, primary and secondary engine nozzle indicators and a centre of gravity meter – but despite diligent searching, there are no flap and slat levers. To the untutored eye it is as foreign and daunting as a cathedral organ is to the tone deaf. But to the crew it is like home; a place that both gives and demands nurture.

'Good morning gentlemen.' It is the Cabin Services director introducing himself to the flight deck crew. The cabin, with the new 'space-age grey' upholstery, has been meticulously checked by the six cabin crew, as has the food and drink to be consumed during the flight. However well the aircraft is operated technically, it is the cabin crew who must supply the ambiance and good feeling that will make the passengers say: 'We had such a good flight . . .' Dedicated to Concorde they meet the challenge. They are lucky since they can see the fruits of their dedication – satisfied passengers. But the cabin crew are trained in other equally vital tasks affecting the well-being of the passengers; they must be experts with all the emergency and survival equipment that is carried on board.

No less dedicated, but behind the scenes, are the thousands of individuals who have made the flight possible. The shifts of engineers, the refuellers, the catering staff, the Chairman, the ramp controller, the Chief

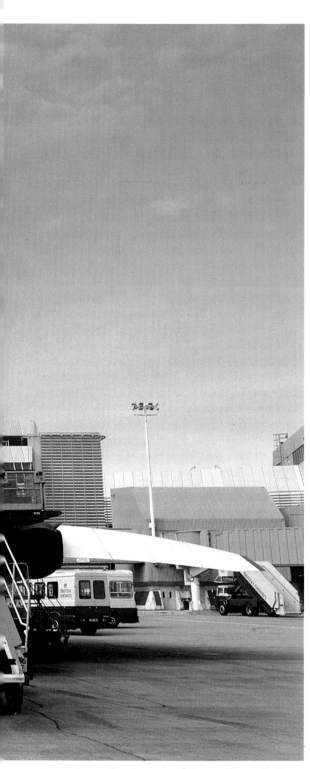

'Number four uplifted four quarts,'

'No performance A.D.D.'s, but there is a history on number two H.F. radio, it is very slow to tune.'

'Speedbird Concorde one nine three, cleared to New York Brecon one foxtrot, squawk two one zero three, track Sierra Mike.'*

'Cleared to start, one two one nine for push'.

The clearance is read back by the crew to the tower.

'Fifty three and half for take-off with a burn-off of 900 kilograms' comes another statement. It is akin to the tuning up of an orchestra.

The Captain or First Officer may fly the aircraft. Today it is the First Officer's turn, so the Captain acts as co-pilot to the First Officer although he retains overall command. Thus the captain reads the 'before start check list'. Henceforward all actions are co-ordinated between the three crew as a team, and each one, where possible, monitors the other's actions.

'Altimeters' says the Captain.

'QNH one zero one five set, eighty, six eighty, normal and 20 ft on the radio altimeter' comes the reply. Later: 'INS one, two and three'. Concorde is navigated by three inertial navigation systems (INS). Once programmed with the latitude and longitude of the starting point of the aircraft, they will continually read out the aircraft's position. Programmed with a route (a series of turning or 'way-points') the auto-pilot will steer the aircraft along that route. All three computers are checked.

'ASI bugs and pitch indices' says the Captain. 'Vee one, one six zero; rotate, one nine five . . .' These are the relevant take-off speeds. The first one, 160 knots, is the decision speed. Up to this speed the aircraft may safely stop within the runway distance; beyond, the take-off may be continued safely even with one of the four engines out of action. On this journey the aircraft will be 'rotated' (that is pitched up) to 13 degrees at 195 knots (225 mph) to become airborne at 217 knots (250 mph).

The loadsheet is checked. Ninety of the one hundred passengers have turned up and are on board; there are ten 'no-shows'. The zero fuel weight and the zero fuel centre of gravity have been programmed into the relevant computer. They are finally checked. Fuel is shifted or 'burnt off' prior to take-off to position the centre of gravity to one specific point. With no tailplane, the precise

*Track 'SM' is the westbound Atlantic supersonic track (see endpapers).

Tail view of Concorde G-BOAE at Terminal Four, Heathrow. The 'elevons' are drooped since, without the engines running, there is no hydraulic pressure; nor is any electric power generated. As Concorde is not fitted with an Auxiliary Power Unit to generate electric power, this has to be supplied from a source on the ground. Note the tailwheel, fitted to avoid the exhaust nozzles of the engines contacting the ground on take-off and landing following an 'over-rotation' (see page 69). The prototypes were fitted with a tail bumper

Executive, the tractor driver, the administrators . . . the list goes on. Their roles are vital, their aim identical – the successful flight of British Airways aircraft. That Concorde performs so well is proof that great pride in the job exists with this section of British Airways. Success breeds success; the 'Halo' effect of Concorde benefits all sections of the airline.

Familiar calls can now be heard.

'OK for boarding?'

'Fuel book,'

Instrument panel during supersonic cruise. Top centre, the selected autopilot modes are lit – horizontal path is defined by the Inertial Navigation System, vertical path by the combined 'Max Climb' and 'Max Cruise' (max of: Mach 2.04, 530 kts (indicated) or stagnation temp of 127°C). A sudden increase of Mach number due to air temperature decrease is contained by the autothrottle switching out of stand-by to decrease thrust (Painting by Roy Huxley)

The pilot's view of the instruments during Mach 2 cruise. At 53,000 ft the indicated airspeed is 501 knots although the true airspeed is 1,150 knots as evidenced by the Machmeter. Concorde climbs gently throughout the cruise as the weight reduces. The rate of climb in this picture is about 500 ft/min

means that the Mach number will rise. At 25,000 ft it will have risen to Mach 0.93 – the limit for a subsonic climb. At that point there will still be about 70 nm to go before the coastline – the acceleration point. Once clear of the coastline, Concorde can accelerate to a Mach number which would cause the sonic boom to be heard. Usually the boom does not reach the surface until Mach 1.15 is achieved, a figure dependent on temperatures and winds.

'Centre of gravity steady at 55 per cent' the Engineer intones. As the Mach number builds the centre of lift starts to move to the rear. This has to be compensated for by the

rearward movement of the centre of gravity by about 2 ft, achieved by shifting the fuel. By the time Mach 2 is reached the centre of gravity will have been moved aft by a further 4 ft.

The autopilot 'acquires' 28,000 ft. As it does so the auto-throttles switch in and take responsibility for maintaining the speed – Mach 0.95 (385 knots indicated airspeed at this altitude), 100 mph faster than most subsonic aircraft.

'Speedbird Concorde one nine three cleared cruise climb, flight level four nine zero to six zero zero.' The message is acknowledged and 60,000 ft is programmed into the autopilot.

'Checks complete down to the afterburners; fuel is going aft; one mile to go,' says the Engineer. The First Officer pushes the throttle fully forward. A signal is sent to the engines, via their controlling computers, to give maximum climb power. The distance 'to go' shows zero.

'Inboard reheats' . . . a nudge as they light up increasing the thrust by about 20 per cent.

'Outboard reheats,' . . . another nudge. Each engine is now burning fuel at over 11 tonnes per hour. The Mach number climbs and hovers on Mach 1. The shock wave passes the static pressure-ports on the side of the fuselage causing a fluctuation on the pressure driven instruments, notably on the vertical speed indicator. Mach 1.01 is indicated and Concorde is supersonic.

At Mach 1.3 the variable ramps inside the engine air intakes begin to operate. They arrange the shock waves formed in the intake mouth in the most efficient pattern possible to compress and slow the airflow down prior to its entering the engine face.

The acceleration becomes more rapid as the Mach number builds. The passengers watch the progress on the 'Marilake' indicators at the front of each cabin. At Mach 1.7 a barely perceptible lurch indicates that the after-burners have been switched off. Reference to the cabin indicators shows the aircraft to be climbing through 43,500 ft, the outside air temperature to be minus 52°C (−62°F) and the ground speed 1,120 mph. There is a 20 mph headwind. Acceleration is now less rapid. Forty minutes from take-off Mach 2 is attained at an altitude of 50,200 ft and lunch is served.

'Ladies and gentlemen, at the risk of interrupting the Marriage of Figaro on the inflight entertainment – or worse still, your conversation,' says the First Officer, 'We are cruising at Mach 2 (a mile every $2\frac{3}{4}$ seconds) and climbing gently towards twice the height of Mount Everest – 58,000 ft. Here at the threshold of space, the sky above is far darker, almost black and the view of the Earth's horizon just betrays the Earth's curvature. Today it is very clear but big

volcanic eruptions in any part of the world, throwing up tons of minute fragments of debris into the upper atmosphere, can reduce the clarity.

'The sun is now climbing from the west. In winter it is possible to leave London after sunset, on the evening Concorde for New York, and watch the sun rise out of the west. Flying at Mach 2 in an easterly direction at these latitudes will cause the sun to set in the west at three times its normal rate, casting, as it does so, a vast curved shadow of the Earth, up and ahead of the aircraft.'

Mercifully the passengers do not choose Concorde solely to observe astronomical phenomena whilst eating haute cuisine served by the dedicated cabin crew. They fly on Concorde because it saves them days, not hours. West-bound, the critical working hours of the day are preserved; east-bound, the purgatory of the overnight sector is avoided. Concorde only flies between London and the United States during the waking hours of the Atlantic Seaboard dwellers.

Two hours out of London, Newfoundland is visible on the right-hand side. The passengers visit the flight deck. Foreign secretaries, famous people, chief executives, pop stars, owners of publishing empires, financiers and Concorde admirers, who have just come to experience 20th-century air travel at its most supreme, are among the

Newfoundland amid stretches of frozen sea from 55,000 ft. The earth's curvature is visible, albeit slightly exaggerated in this picture. The sky above is almost black here on the threshold of space

• The radiation metre is visible on the lower right of the panel
Senior Engineer Officer Bill Johnstone demonstrating that the gap to the rear of the engineer's panel is wide enough to accommodate a hand when the fuselage has expanded, due to its having been heated by the airflow at Mach 2.

passengers. All are treated as VIPs.

Some are stunned into silence. Then 'Do you know what each of these switches and dials do?' 'No,' replies the First Officer, 'We only have them to preserve the mystique,' laughter, then: 'Does Concorde really grow eight inches during the cruise?'

The engineer explains that due to the compression and friction of the air, the temperature of the outer surface of the fuselage rises to about 100°C (212°F), hence the expansion and increase in length. He puts his hand into a gap between his panel and bulkhead; it fits. 'Once the fuselage is cool there is no space to do that. If you want two flights on Concorde leave your hand there during the deceleration, it will become trapped. The only way then of removing it would be to wait for the next supersonic flight. It would be painful, but it might be worth it!' he adds with a grin.

Should the temperature on the nose, the hottest point, be about to exceed 127°C (260°F), then the Mach number has to be reduced. This occurs when the outside air temperature becomes warmer than minus 50°C (−58°F). The speed of sound is greater in warmer air so the reduced Mach number has little effect on the flight time.

'Boston this is Speedbird Concorde one nine three heavy flight level five six eight.' (56,800 feet.) A small cross with BA 193, FL 568 and 999 appears on the controllers radar screen. The 999 refers to Concorde's ground speed, the radar is calibrated no higher, so cannot show the 1,120 knots registered in the cockpit.

'Speedbird Concorde one nine three heavy. Roger. I have you radar identified. Omit position reports.' (The suffix 'heavy' serves to differentiate groups of aircraft, on the basis of maximum allowable take-off weight.)

Concorde is passing the south-western end of Nova Scotia now. The track is being precisely steered by the autopilot following instructions from the inertial navigation system (INS). A small yellow light captioned 'R Nav' illuminates in the top right hand corner of the Captain's instrument panel. Nantucket DME (distance measuring equipment – a radio pulse beacon), over 250 nm away, has just taken over the refinement of the almost impeccable accuracy of the inertial navigation system. Travelling at 1,900 ft per second the position is known to within about 2,000 ft.

The end of the supersonic cruise is near.

Engine instruments on the centre panel. Each vertical row of five gauges applies to one engine, there are yet more on the engineer's panel. Note the fuel flows, they total about 20 tonnes/hr. To the lower right, the INS shows the position in latitude and longitude. The left hand one shows distance to go to the next turning point and the time to go in minutes, 334 nm in 18.5 minutes. Gander DME, (refining the INS position) was 176.1 nm to the north when the picture was taken, as shown by the readout on the right of the picture. Note the readings of temperature, altitude, indicated airspeed and Mach number

CONCORDE

Concorde has a cabin crew of six, and their dedication to Concorde has been fundamental to the success of commercial supersonic flight. Here they are shown wearing the uniform current at Concorde's tenth anniversary with British Airways – 21st January 1986. The menu and Flight Certificate on the right are of the same date

MACH 2·00

Some of the snippets of information appearing in the 'Marilake' passenger display screens placed on the bulkhead to the front of each of the cabins. During the cruise the Mach number is 2.00; from time to time the plasma screens show the distance to go derived from the aircraft's navigation system (See top photograph on page 92)

WELCOME
TO
CONCORDE

TEMP
−11°C

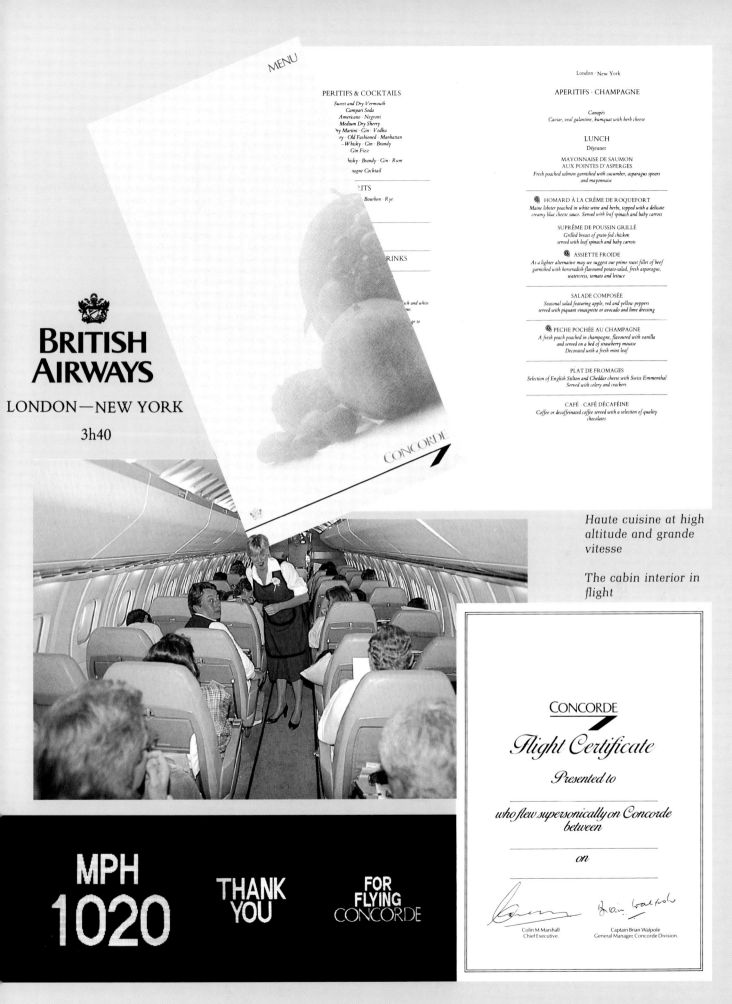

MENU

PERITIFS & COCKTAILS

Sweet and Dry Vermouth
Campari Soda
Americano · Negroni
Medium Dry Sherry
Dry Martini · Gin · Vodka
Dry · Old Fashioned · Manhattan
Whisky · Gin · Brandy
Gin Fizz

Whisky · Brandy · Gin · Rum

Champagne Cocktail

SPIRITS

Bourbon · Rye

DRINKS

London · New York

APERITIFS · CHAMPAGNE

Canapés
Caviar, veal galantine, kumquat with herb cheese

LUNCH
Déjeuner

MAYONNAISE DE SAUMON
AUX POINTES D'ASPERGES
Fresh poached salmon garnished with cucumber, asparagus spears
and mayonnaise

HOMARD À LA CRÈME DE ROQUEFORT
Maine lobster poached in white wine and herbs, topped with a delicate
creamy blue cheese sauce. Served with leaf spinach and baby carrots

SUPRÊME DE POUSSIN GRILLÉ
Grilled breast of grain-fed chicken
served with leaf spinach and baby carrots

ASSIETTE FROIDE
As a lighter alternative may we suggest our prime roast fillet of beef
garnished with horseradish-flavoured potato-salad, fresh asparagus,
watercress, tomato and lettuce

SALADE COMPOSÉE
Seasonal salad featuring apple, red and yellow peppers
served with piquant vinaigrette or avocado and lime dressing

PECHE POCHÉE AU CHAMPAGNE
A fresh peach poached in champagne, flavoured with vanilla
and served on a bed of strawberry mousse
Decorated with a fresh mint leaf

PLAT DE FROMAGES
Selection of English Stilton and Cheddar cheese with Swiss Emmenthal
Served with celery and crackers

CAFÉ · CAFÉ DÉCAFÉINE
Coffee or decaffeinated coffee served with a selection of quality
chocolates

CONCORDE

BRITISH AIRWAYS

LONDON—NEW YORK

3h40

Haute cuisine at high
altitude and grande
vitesse

The cabin interior in
flight

MPH 1020

THANK YOU

FOR FLYING CONCORDE

CONCORDE

Flight Certificate

Presented to

_____

*who flew supersonically on Concorde
between*

_____

on

_____

Colin M Marshall
Chief Executive.

Captain Brian Walpole
General Manager, Concorde Division.

97

The Flight – Deceleration

The view through the visor at speeds greater than 250 knots. Once the angle of attack is less than 9°, vision ahead is no longer obscured by the nose and visor in the fully up position, as shown here. The view is excellent in comparison to the view through the periscopic device fitted to the prototypes which only had a diminutive transparent visor as shown on the model Concorde on page 50

'Speedbird Concorde one nine three heavy, Boston, cross three nine four three north seven one zero seven west at flight level five two zero or above, cleared to cross Linnd flight level three nine zero or above. Descend and maintain flight level three nine zero.' The descent clearance is read back. Concorde must cross the boundary of a 'warning' area, dedicated to military flying, above 52,000 ft, before entering the regular airways system at a point over the ocean called Linnd at 39,000 ft or above, but no lower – yet.

The deceleration and descent distance is calculated; typically 120 nm are covered from Mach 2 to Mach 1. Decelerating over the ocean en route to New York, the point at which the deceleration is started is dictated by the distance required for nearly the whole descent. On most other routes it is fixed by the need to be subsonic 35 nm before any coastline sensitive to sonic booms; on those occasions Concorde decelerates through Mach 1 level at 41,000 ft;

into New York Concorde becomes subsonic during the descent through 35,000 ft.

There is a sharp noise: it is a microchip's rendering of a 'wake-up!' bugle call. The crew are carrying out the 'Deceleration and Descent Checklist'. The first item is to test the warnings associated with the autopilot disconnecting itself – hence the alerting audio warning. Next come the radio aids required for the landing and the procedure for climbing out again, if the landing is aborted for any reason. The altitude to which it is safe to descend and the whereabouts of the high ground or buildings are scrutinised. Finally the crew adjust their safety harnesses.

'Ladies and gentlemen, in 200 miles – 10 minutes in Concorde, but half an hour for the Boeing 747 in the 100 knot headwind which it is experiencing beneath us – we shall be commencing our deceleration. The time in New York is twenty past eight in the morning. We shall be landing at five past nine, on runway four right – the right hand of the two north-east facing runways. The rain has cleared and the temperature is 70°F.'

Thrust is reduced to an intermediate setting. Too low a value might cause the engines to surge (backfire); alarming, but not dangerous; also the racks of computers would overheat if the air conditioning supplied by the engines failed to supply a sufficient cooling draught.

There is a whiff of ozone. Between 40,000 ft and 60,000 ft Concorde has been flying in an ozone rich atmosphere. At 'cruise power' the compression of the air in the engines heats the air to over 400°C (750°F). This converts all the ozone present in the compressor into oxygen. The air bled from the engines prior to its being cooled in the air conditioning system is thus free of ozone. At reduced power, the compression and heating are less – hence the trace of ozone. In spite of the huge temperature drop in the supply of air to the air conditioning system, there is no temperature variation in the cabin.

At Mach 1.6 there is a further thrust reduction. Once the indicated airspeed has dropped to 350 knots the descent commences: 350 knots at 58,000 ft corresponds to a Mach number of 1.55 (890 knots true airspeed); by 35,000 ft it will correspond to Mach 1*.

The engineer moves the centre of gravity forward to keep the aircraft in trim. He pumps fuel from a tank in the rear of the

aircraft to tanks in the fuselage and wings. Eight or nine tonnes of fuel are moved forward at this stage. The gap between his panel and the bulkhead closes and the warmth radiating from the windows reduces as the fuselage cools.

Further descent clearance is acknowledged: 'Roger New York, cross three five miles south-east of Sates at one two thousand feet, altimeter two nine eight four.' The altimeters are adjusted to show altitude referenced to the pressure at sea level, 29.84 inches of

The author on the flight deck of Concorde 002, now at Yeovilton, showing the original visor/heat shield in the 'up' position. Even with a periscopic device to improve forward vision, the US Federal Aviation Administration would not have certificated this arrangement. Concorde subsequently benefited from improved glazing techniques

The three crew members at work. In the foreground is Senior Flight Engineer George Floyd

*See the 'Flight envelope' in Appendix.

mercury. Hitherto, they have shown altitude referenced to a standard pressure of 29.92 inches of mercury (1,013.25 millibars) – hence the instruction to maintain 'flight levels'. A flight level of 350 corresponds to 35,000 feet with the altimeter referenced to the standard pressure setting of 1013.25 millibars.

'Concorde one nine three, traffic eleven o'clock five miles south-west bound – one one thousand feet.' The crew peer slightly left and below. 'Contact, Speedbird Concorde one nine three.' 'Contact' means that the other aircraft has been seen – nothing worse. Although air traffic controllers are primarily responsible for the separation of aircraft under their charge, the crew include a careful lookout as part of their cockpit routine. The view ahead, although the visor is raised, is surprisingly good.

As the speed falls the angle of attack must be increased to maintain the lift. 'Angle of attack' is not some kind of refined military manoeuvre; it is the angle between the aircraft and the oncoming air (see page 11). As it is increased so the view of the airspace directly ahead of the pilots becomes progressively obscured by the nose. By 250 knots the visor and nose must be lowered for adequate vision ahead to be maintained. Initially the nose is lowered to five degrees. On final approach, where the angle of attack is 14 degrees, the nose is lowered to its fully down position (12.5 degrees).

'All secure aft,' the chief steward reports. This means that he has checked that all the passengers are strapped in and the cabin equipment is stowed ready for landing.

'Ladies and gentlemen, this is the First Officer. We are under the control of the New York radar controller and will be landing in eight minutes from now.'

'Speedbird Concorde one nine three, fly heading three five zero degrees to establish on the localiser runway four right, maintain 2,000 ft until established, reduce to two one zero knots.' The instruction is acknowledged, and the aircraft turns while 210 knots is dialled into the 'auto-throttles' and the 'IAS acq' button is pressed. As the speed falls below 220 knots the drag increases, calling for a thrust increase. Concorde is unique among airliners in flying at speeds below its minimum drag speed.

A short 'bugle call' is heard. The First Officer has disconnected the autopilot. Today he will carry out a manual landing. 'Localiser active,' calls the Captain. The radio beam defining the path to follow to the runway has been approached. The aircraft must be turned to the right from its heading of 350° M (referenced to Magnetic north) onto one that will let it track precisely along the radio beam transmitted from the ground. There is a crosswind from the right so the aircraft heads 48° M (3° east of north-east) to track 43° M along the localiser beam of runway 4 R.

By 12 miles to touchdown the speed has been stabilised at 190 knots. 'Glideslope active,' calls the Captain. There are 9 miles to touch down. 'Gear down and landing check-list please,' calls the First Officer. The engineer reads the checklist. There is a double thump as the main undercarriage legs lock down, almost simultaneously. Four green lights appear confirming that all four have been extended – two main, one nose and a tail gear.

Visor and nose in up position

Visor down with nose at 5 degrees. The 'pitot' tube on the tip of the nose senses 'dynamic' pressure to measure airspeed. To the rear of a second pitot tube, halfway along the nose, is an incidence vane to measure, after compensation for the droop angle of the nose, the 'angle of attack'

'Nose,' says the engineer.

'Down and green,' replies the Captain, referring, not to the colour of the nose, but to a green light which confirms that the nose is locked down. The view of the runway is now quite unobscured.

'Glideslope engaged,' calls the Captain. Concorde will now follow a second radio beam, this one slopes towards the landing point making an angle of three degrees with the horizontal. Together the two radio beams, glideslope and localiser, are called the Instrument Landing System (ILS). The word 'glide' here is a misnomer. No jet aircraft could glide at such a shallow angle to the horizontal with all the drag from its flaps, least of all Concorde, with the high 'induced' drag found when the slender delta wings are asked to give lift at slow speed. It is a powered approach. A speed of 190 knots is maintained through use of the auto-throttles.

The First Officer follows two yellow bars which form a cross over his artificial horizon. The horizontal one commands him to pitch the aircraft either up or down to maintain the 'glideslope'; the vertical one, to turn either left or right to follow the 'localiser'. The bars are signalled by the automatic flight control system. Had the autopilot been engaged it would have pitched and turned the aircraft to follow the two radio beams.

'One thousand foot radio,' calls the Flight Engineer. This is the height of the main-wheels above the surface, determined by bouncing a radio wave off the surface. It is a far more precise measurement of height than that available through the pressure alti-meter; however, it only works below 2,500 ft. So well does it measure the height of the aircraft above the ground that the aircraft performs incredibly smooth automatic land-ings, somewhat to the chagrin of the pilots.

'Beep, Beep, BEEP, BEEP, Beep, Beep' in the headsets.

'Marker, height checks,' says the Captain. This is in response to this audible radio beacon being overflown at the correct height – 920 ft. The veracity of the glideslope has been checked – a little academic with the runway so clearly in view, but vital in conditions of low visibility.

'Eight hundred feet radio,' calls the Flight Engineer. Now the speed is reduced from 190 knots to the speed required just over the threshold of the runway, 163 knots at a landing weight of 103 tonnes. Concorde decelerates during the descent from 800 ft (2.34 nm before touchdown) to 500 ft (1.34 nm before touchdown). To maintain 163 knots, more power is required than was needed at 190 knots. The procedure is called the 'reduced noise approach', because less thrust is needed throughout the approach down to 500 ft. First because the drag is less

Opposite The Flight Engineer's panel showing the fuel management system. In the centre there is the centre of gravity metre showing 58.8 per cent (a measure of its position with respect to the Aerodynamic Root Reference Chord – see page 106), half way along the chord would be 50 per cent; one per cent corresponds to about one foot. The white pointer must lie within the two orange limit pointers (marked FWD and AFT) in order to maintain aerodynamic balance. The tank at the rear has 9,810 kg of fuel in it. This will be moved forward to central tanks during the deceleration. The total fuel on board is showing 34,000 kg. In this picture each engine has used about 15,000 kg

View of runway 4R
at JFK from about
1000 ft on final
approach over the
lowered nose and
visor

—200 feet —

—*100 feet*—

Crossing the runway threshold. The wheels are still at 50 ft above the ground with the pilots another 37 ft above them

Training
of the Concorde Pilot

—100 feet—

Crossing the runway threshold. The wheels are still at 50 ft above the ground with the pilots another 37 ft above them at 190 knots than at 163 knots and secondly because less thrust is required during the period of deceleration. The noise generated by the engines is less with less thrust, and the fuel consumption is lower. Had an automatic landing been carried out, the final approach speed would have been achieved by 1,200 ft above the surface, so stabilising the descent rate for a longer period to allow the landing computer to make a smooth touchdown.

During final approach Concorde consumes fuel at ten times the rate per mile than is the case towards the latter end of the supersonic cruise. At the intermediate speeds the fuel consumption is also much higher; hence the requirement to arrive with 15 tonnes of spare fuel, enough for 50 minutes in the stacking pattern prior to a landing.

'Speedbird Concorde one nine three heavy, cleared to land four right wind zero seven zero at one five knots,' says the controller in the Kennedy tower. Rarely is

Concorde held up by congestion at this hour in the morning.

'Cleared to land Speedbird Concorde one nine three heavy,' acknowledges the Captain.

'Five hundred feet,' calls the Flight Engineer. It is somewhat reminiscent of a 19th century sailor calling out the depths he has plumbed ('By the mark ten').

'Stabilised', confirms the Captain. The auto-throttles have captured the final approach speed – 163 knots and Concorde is established in the correct position for landing.

'Four hundred feet,'

'One hundred to go,' responds the Captain

'Three hundred feet,'

'Decision height,' calls the Captain.

Landing clearance has been received, the runway is visible and clear of obstacles. 'Continuing,' responds the First Officer. A 'go-around' is possible right up to the point of touchdown.

The approach lights on runway four right

protrude out of the water of Jamaica Bay. 'Two hundred feet,' and the pilots are 37 ft higher than the main wheels. 'One hundred feet'; over dry land now. 'Fifty', the auto-throttles are disconnected. 'Forty, thirty, twenty, fifteen.' The throttles are manually closed. At this point the aircraft would be pitched forward, both by the pressure of air trapped between it and the runway, referred to as 'ground effect', and by the reduction in thrust, but the First Officer gently checks this tendency by bringing the control column back to hold the attitude constant as the descent rate decays in the increasing ground effect. He also pushes the left rudder pedal to lose the remaining three degrees of drift required to fly down the centre of the runway, caused by the crosswind. Now the main wheels track along the runway for a moment before the touch.

A puff of smoke and dust whisks from each set of main-wheel tyres into the two vortices, one over each wing: a clear indication of the nature of the airflow that has been supplying lift during the final stages of the approach. Idle reverse thrust is selected whilst the next manoeuvre is carried out – landing the nose wheel; during this the flight deck has to descend a further 17 ft.

'Stick forward,' calls the First Officer. The nose-wheel is down, and reverse thrust is selected. There is a roar in the cabin – noisier than at take-off. The brakes are applied. The stopping appears urgent, but all is normal. 'One hundred knots,' calls the Captain. Outboard engines are selected to idle reverse. 'Seventy five knots', and the inboards go to idle reverse. 'Forty knots groundspeed,' all engines are selected to forward idle thrust.

'After landing check, shut down two and three,' says the First Officer. The nose is selected to five degrees, unnecessary systems are switched off, the two inboard engines are shut down and the Engineer pumps four tonnes of fuel into the front tank to ensure that the aircraft will not tip tail down during unloading.

'Left at the end, cross one three left, right on the outer and call ground point nine,' says the controller. It is a kind of pidgin English, meaningless to the uniniated, but totally clear to the crew. Over the maze of concrete and tarmac that constitutes John F Kennedy Airport, New York, the crew find their way to the British Airways Terminal, at a speed no faster than a mile every two and three quarter minutes.

'Ladies and gentlemen, welcome to New York.' This time it is the Captain addressing the passengers.

'Our maximum altitude today was 58,000 ft and our maximum speed 1,320 mph, giving an average over the whole distance of close on 1,100 mph. On behalf of all the crew thank you for flying with us on Concorde; we look forward to seeing you all again. Finally, the Jumbo jet that left 10 minutes before us from Heathrow is very nearly, but not quite, half way here.'

A marshaller waving two fluorescent wands directs Concorde over the last few feet. The wands cross, the aircraft stops.

'Parking checklist,' says the First Officer.
'Brakes,' responds the Engineer.
'To park,' replies the First Officer.
The checklist continues, like some litany. The passengers disembark. 'Mind your head sir as you leave' cautions the Cabin Services Director, standing at the forward door to bid 'au revoir' to the passengers. They have had an excellent flight.

The landing sequence. Concorde G-BOAF landing on runway 4R at Kennedy. Note the vortices, the landing of the nosewheel and the buckets (secondary nozzles) closed over the jet pipes to deflect the jet efflux forward at an angle of about 50° to the horizontal to give reverse thrust. Since the aircraft tends to pitch up with reverse thrust selected the stick is held forward, thus the elevons move down, as can be seen. The nose is in its fully down (12½°) position for the landing, once the landing run is complete it is selected to 5°

Training of the Concorde Pilot

British Airways, like most of the world's airlines, only employs pilots who are already qualified. They must have at least a Commercial Pilot's Licence (CPL), be rated to fly a twin-engined aircraft and have an Instrument Rating. The latter allows a pilot to fly an appropriately equipped aircraft in cloud and into certain types of 'controlled' airspace, whether or not he can rely on visual reference. A private individual can pay for his (or her) own training at a CAA (Civil Aviation Authority) 'approved' flying college – a very expensive procedure (£55,000 1993 price at Prestwick). Or he can become qualified by acquiring 700 flying hours (200 hrs on the 'approved' course) and passing the relevant exams. Although cheaper, the 700-hour route to a professional licence can take several years.

If he (which includes 'she' in this chapter) is lucky, he may find that airlines in general, and BA in particular, are recruiting cadet pilots. If this is the case he can apply for BA sponsorship at one of the CAA 'approved' flying colleges. For this there are certain criteria: typically he must be between 18 and 24 years old at the start of training, be medically fit and be predicted to stay that way during his career (up to 55 in BA, but 60 is the UK upper age limit for most commercial flying). Furthermore, he must have the necessary exam qualifications and pass the interviews, along with co-ordination and aptitude tests. Usually, the exam qualifications include two 'A' levels, preferably physics and maths, but he must have passed at least maths and a science subject, along with English and two others at GCSE. A University degree may waive some of the specific requirements described above.

The next hurdle for the sponsored pilot is to successfully complete the 56-week CAA 'approved' course. Following the sale of the BA College of Air Training at Hamble, near Southampton, in 1987, BA has sent most of its cadet pilots to the British Aerospace

Training on the simulator of the two-crew Boeing 747-400. Concorde, in spite of being more complex, was developed just before information presented in cockpits via television screens became common place. Outside, the computer-generated image of the runway at night is stunningly realistic

Proof of motivation is essential for any pilot seeking training sponsorship from an airline. However, basic training does not include hang-gliding. Delta wing gliders of the 1920s were developed to reduce drag. On this descendant at the Grand Salève near Geneva, the upturned wing tips restore the stability normally provided by a tailplane. The effectiveness of swept wings for flight close to Mach 1 was not recognised until World War 2

School at Prestwick in Scotland.

Once in the airline, the BA pilot can choose, within certain constraints such as seniority, the type of aircraft that he wants to fly. If that aircraft should be Concorde certain extra rules apply. He must already have been qualified on one of BA's aircraft, which means in practice he would have been in the airline for at least three years. He must, in order to justify the extra training expense, be able to serve sufficient years before promotion or retirement.

There are four main parts to any conversion course: 1) the technical course, plus written examinations; 2) the simulator course, plus compulsory tests; 3) 'Base' training – flying the aircraft without passengers – also with tests; and 4) flying under supervision with passengers, plus the final 'route' check. The pilot then becomes fully qualified to fly as Captain or Co-pilot.

During the six-week Concorde technical course for pilots (eight for Flight Engineers), each system – hydraulics, electrics, flying controls and undercarriage – has to be thoroughly learnt. On the B747-400 this course lasts a mere three weeks. The information for most aircraft conversion courses in BA since the 1970s is presented through means of an 'audio visual' – slides accompanied by audio tapes. On Concorde the 'audio' part is taken by a lecturer, which allows dialogue that can highlight, for instance, how a system evolved – a helpful element in the learning process. During the Concorde technical course the simulator is

The model airport with a 'flying' TV camera like this one for the Concorde simulator at Filton has been superseded by a computer which can generate images of all the main airports. In the original Concorde simulator set up, data for the radio beacons around various airports included those of Novosibirsk, in Russia. Had the TU 144 been a success, a one-stop trans-Siberian route to Tokyo might have been negotiated for Concorde

The Concorde trainee on the simulator can find himself viewing a computer-generated image of the high rise blocks on the hills of Hong Kong (seen here) then, travelling apparently at a small percentage of the speed of light, arrive in New York, complete with a view of the World Trade Centre. Clever optics places the 165° panorama at infinity

used as a 'systems trainer', illustrating theory with simulated practice. Finally, the CAA-administered exam takes the form of a multichoice test on each system.

On Concorde the simulator training lasts 76 hours – 19 4-hour details (50 hours are spent on the B747-400). Every emergency procedure is practised until perfect. Single or double engine failure, pressurisation failure followed by emergency descent and failure of electrical signalling to the flying controls, are examples of some of the procedures. The trainee must pass several tests on the simulator. Finally, he has to renew his Instrument Rating – the general qualification which is not normally specific to a particular aircraft type.

The visual and motion systems on some aircraft simulators qualify the converting pilot to demonstrate his first landing on that aircraft for real with passengers on

board – albeit under the supervision of a highly experienced training Captain. Originally the Concorde simulator (at Filton, Bristol) made use of a television camera 'flying' (suspended) over a model runway and environs within circuit distance. The image captured was projected onto a screen in front of the cockpit, but only with a limited horizontal field of vision, albeit collimated to infinity. By 1989 the original system had been replaced by a 150° field of view, colour, daylight, dusk or night computer-generated image. It is capable of showing individual airports, like Hong Kong with its famous curved approach path, or London Heathrow complete with gasometer to the north east as well as the airport buildings – to give realism during taxying. In addition, the Concorde trainee must carry out about 15 landings during 'base' training. On the B747-400, only if the pilot's previous type has been significantly different from the Boeing, must he land the real aircraft, usually a minimum of four times.

Take-off in the real Concorde, (like the simulator), is commenced with the call, 'Three, two, one, now' when the throttles are moved smoothly and swiftly from their idle position to fully open. The bank of engine gauges react with whirling digits and a single synchronised swing of 20 needles. Next, the four primary nozzle area gauges move into the white segment, proof that each reheat has lit. The brightness of the outside and the force of the acceleration are evidence that this is no simulator. Each Concorde pilot flies three 'details' totalling 2¾ hour (½ hour at night) and carries out at least 14 circuits. Most are 'touch and go's' (landing without stopping followed by immediate take-off), while a few will be 'go arounds' (approach to less than 200 ft above the runway followed by a climb out). On about half a dozen occasions there is a simulated loss of thrust from one engine on take-off. Once all the items are satisfactorily completed, the pilot is on to the final stage – route flying.

Now the trainee, under supervision and with an extra crew member to 'cover' for him, operates his first scheduled supersonic sectors. To begin with on the flight deck there hardly seems to be enough time to fit in all the pre-departure tasks: Air Traffic Control clearance, take-off calculations, check lists, briefings, loadsheet, technical log, the problems caused by a late passenger, a minor technical defect – is there time to correct it, or does it limit performance? Relief at last, the door closes and it is time to depart. At least the flying is not so different from that received during training – confidence returns.

As the sectors clock up, so the tasks seem to require less time. Finally at the end of 20 sectors for a Captain and 16 for a First Officer the 'route' check is carried out. Once successfully over this last hurdle, the pilot suffers no more formal supervision. He is now qualified until the next six-month check on the simulator and the next annual 'route' check on the aircraft. On average six months elapse from the start to finish of a Concorde course, in comparison to about three-and-a-half months for the B747-400.

In April 1993 the first woman pilot ever to be qualified on Concorde took to the supersonic routes, Barbara Harmer, a former British Caledonian pilot, becoming a Concorde First Officer. By December 1993 99 BA pilots and 38 flight engineers had successfully completed the Concorde conversion course.

Excellent though the simulator is, the trainee Concorde pilot must fly at least 14 circuits before his/her route training. At high angles of attack – 14° on final approach to landing – drag increases (demanding extra thrust) with reducing speed. Experiencing both the 'feel' of the actual aircraft, and the look of the runway in reality, arms the pilot with the confidence needed to tackle his/her first landing with passengers

In April 1993 Senior First Officer Barbara Harmer became Concorde's first lady pilot. Hairdressing, private flying, air traffic controlling, flying instructing to grant of Commercial Pilot's and joining British Caledonian, gave Barbara the eligibility to 'bid' for a Concorde course after 'BCal's' merger with BA in 1987

The Future

Concorde represents a significant technological achievement. During development it extended the frontiers of aeronautical knowledge. In terms of supersonic hours flown it has comfortably outstripped the combined airforces of the world. Flying into its third decade of operation it still has a substantial portion of its life before it. Concorde has become, as the French say, 'engravé sur le marbre' (engraved on the marble). Concorde represents a real point on the graph of aeronautical progress, not an estimate of where an SST might have been, had one been developed in the 1960s. Such faith has British Airways in its flagship leading it into the next millenium, that, at the time of writing (1994), a multimillion pound Concorde refurbishment programme is under way.

The project also proved that international aeronautical collaboration could work, albeit somewhat ponderously. An evolved example of the Concorde experience is the Airbus Industrie consortium at Toulouse, producing a family of subsonic airliners, in which France plays a leading role. Concorde, as the French had hoped, restored their pre-eminence in aviation. Airbus consists of Aerospatiale (France 37.9%), Deutsche Aerospace Airbus (Germany 37.9%), BAe (UK 20%) and CASA (Spain 4.2%).

Concorde in 1962 was supposed to be Britain's entry ticket into the Common Market. Owing to the Polaris missile treaty, General de Gaulle (then President of France) vetoed Britain's entry, regarding its 'Special Relationship' with the United States as being contrary to the European ideal. Whether Britain's entry in 1971 caused the political problems that beset Concorde's entry into the US is open to question, but the UK seemed to have fallen between two political stools. Happily, since then Concorde flights to New York and Washington have enhanced the 'Special Relationship'. Nevertheless, there are lessons here for the future.

Whatever Concorde's technical merits, and they were legion, vast sales of the partner countries' cherished supersonic fledgling were not forthcoming. Only 14 aircraft were sold, and these were to Air France and

Concorde G-BOAG, The Red Arrows and the QE2 over the English Channel, Summer 1985. Captain John Hutchinson, noted for BBC television commentary for major British Air Shows, was on board on this occasion, with Captain Leney (Flight Manager, Technical) at the controls. Very many Concorde charters have been organised by Cunard – hence the publicity value of this association

Right
Until there is a computer powerful enough so that each molecule of air flowing over an airframe can be electronically represented, wind tunnel testing will be essential. Here a British Aerospace AST model is under scrutiny

Far right
Artist's impression of the British Aerospace AST, perhaps a 300 seater of 300 tonnes. Note the canard, the arrow delta layout (as seen on port wing)

and the separate engine pod installations. The elevons will give 'flap' effect thanks to their moving down in compensation to the up lift from the canard and rearward centre of gravity. The arrow delta and separate nacelles generate less drag than the arrangement on Concorde. Advanced optics might allow the nose to be fixed, rather than moveable as in the Concorde

Since the development of Concorde was started in the early 1960s, computers have revolutionised design techniques, replacing armies of draughtsmen. This computer generated image illustrates an Aerospatiale proposal, here without a canard

Various American AST designs based on the 'Arrow' planform. Note the preference for a tailplane, European designs favour a canard

British Airways. One contemporary cartoonist showed a wine glass being held aloft with the caption; 'Cheers, we have sold Concorde to ourselves'.

The failure to sell this technological wonder to the world's airlines has bestowed on British Airways and Air France a unique commercial advantage. The Concorde symbol has become a potent advertising tool for both the British and French flag carriers.

Concorde is exemplary in its prime role. By saving the trans-Atlantic business man the hours of the day, it saves him the days of the week. Westward Concorde beats the clock by an hour, and thus the whole of the first day can be devoted to useful work. Eastward it avoids the purgatory of the disturbed subsonic night, delivering him mentally refreshed for his first day's work in Europe.

The charter world was quick to spot Concorde's attractiveness. First, just as an end in itself – an individual could be wafted up to the threshold of space, all while enjoying champagne and caviare, before being returned to the point of origin. Secondly, as a time machine, transporting the traveller back 4000 years in just three hours from London or Paris, with, for example, a visit to the Pyramids at Gizeh in Egypt. Cunard, for another, noted that there are just two great ways of crossing the Atlantic, QE2 being one and Concorde the other. Roughly a tenth of Concorde's revenue in BA service comes from charter activities.

According to a 1991 Boeing forecast, the number of international passengers will increase from 1.09m per day in the year 2000 to 1.90m passengers per day in 2015. This suggests a potential of 315,000 supersonic passengers per day in 2000, rising to 607,000 by 2015. If each 300-seat Concorde successor flew two sectors per day, there would be a market for 500 aircraft, eventually rising to 1000. The pacific 'rim' is expected to exceed the average growth – an ideal area for a second generation Concorde with its long over water routes insensitive to the sonic boom. The journey time between, for instance, Los Angeles to Tokyo (c 4900 nms) would be reduced from over ten hours to just over four, a fact in itself that would stimulate the market. So what are the prospects for Concorde's successor?

Concorde's design would have evolved had more than 14 'production' aircraft been built. The successor, let us call it the AST (Advanced Supersonic Transport), will be a new design, based on the experience gained

Douglas Aircraft Company

NASA Langley Research & Vought Corporation

Lockheed SCV concept

Fig. 19

with Concorde, allied to the advances made since the mid 1970s. Although no metal has been cut, studies on how to build a better Concorde have been continual, and by the mid 1990s are beginning to look more practical. In April 1994 Aerospatiale, British Aerospace and Deutsche Aerospace announced their intention to work together on research into the possibility of a future supersonic airline. The three key areas for improvement are aerodynamics, propulsion and structure.

The Breguet range equation (see appendix) states that the range of an aircraft is proportional to its aerodynamic efficiency (L/D – Lift to Drag ratio), the higher the bet-

Although twice the take-off weight of Concorde, this design would carry four times the number of passengers. Plans for another version, unveiled in 1989 by Aerospatiale, suggested that a 200 seater AST with a 5400 nm range could soon become commercially viable

Two designs for an AST. The upper version carrying 275 passengers, the lower, 400. Note the presence of a canard. As the design weight exceeds about 650,000 lb, engine silencing becomes progressively more difficult, unless a variable cycle engine is developed

A Lego representative and the author with a Lego model of Concorde beside Concorde G-BOAF at Billund, Denmark, 5 July 1985. Concorde is chartered to many places, this one was to 'Legoland', taking 60 children who had won prizes to see that famous village. One winning entry: 'A flight of my fancy to the land of fancy'

ter; its speed, the faster the better; divided by the rate of fuel that it must use to give a specified thrust (SFC – specific fuel consumption), the lower the better; all this is multiplied by its structural efficiency. The final term is a measure of how much fuel can be made available for the least structural weight of the aircraft, the greater the better.

The lift to drag ratio (L/D) must be improved across the whole speed range. During the Mach 2 cruise on Concorde it is 7.5 and at subsonic cruising speed, Mach 0.95, about 12. At take-off and landing speeds the L/D is a mere 4 in contrast to about 9 on a subsonic passenger jet. This poor L/D is thanks to the generation of lift by vortices over the delta wing – a very effective means of producing lift without flaps and slats, but bought at the expense of enormous drag. Concorde must carry 12-15 tonnes of reserve and diversion fuel for a 10 tonne payload. A Boeing 747 carries a similar reserve for a 50 tonne payload.

The supersonic L/D can be improved by

reshaping the wing into an 'arrow delta' – bringing forward the centre rear portion of a standard delta wing. Control in pitch would be restored by having an extra aerodynamic surface – either a canard (foreplane) or a tailplane. All studies suggest that an L/D in excess of 10 is possible.

An improved low speed L/D would enhance the take-off performance and allow a steeper climb out with less thrust, resulting in less noise and lower fuel burn. On Concorde it costs a ton to carry an extra ton of payload and/or fuel. Requiring less fuel to carry the reserve fuel would translate into a highly favourable improvement in range and/or payload.

The improvement would come from high lift devices, retractable slats along the leading edge of the wing, as fitted to a subsonic airliner, and by making the elevons give flap effect. The 'pitch down' caused by the elevons giving flap effect would be counteracted by a combination of the extra aerodynamic surface (fore- or tail-plane), and by having the centre of gravity situated further

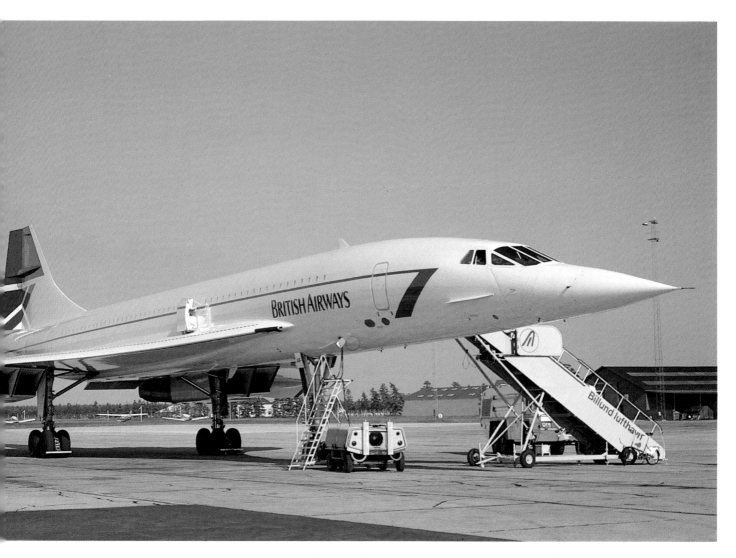

to the rear. A rearward centre of gravity decreases the stability of an aircraft. However 'active controls', pioneered on Concorde, which move the control surfaces independently of the pilot, can artificially restore the stability. This motion is actioned by computers fed with information from accelerometers, and by data concerning the aircraft's airspeed and altitude.

The Wright brothers first aircraft was unstable. It was controllable (just), thanks to the slowness of the unstable pitching. A jet propelled delta winged aircraft would not be so forgiving. Therefore, complete instability, as on the latest fighter aircraft, is not envisaged for the AST. However, absence of an emergency mechanical signalling channel to the flying controls, as on Concorde, would save weight. Thus at least two of, the say four, signalling channels would use fibre optic signalling ('fly-by-light'), which is less vulnerable from a lightning strike than an electrical channel ('fly-by-wire'). Incidentally, starting with a centre of gravity further aft, less fuel would

have to be pumped back to compensate for the rearward movement of the centre of lift during transonic acceleration, enabling the rear tank to be used for storing more fuel at the outset.

A side stick, replacing the conventional control column, was test flown on, but not retrofitted to, the production Concorde. However, it represented the prototype of the kind of controls found on the 'fly-by-wire' Airbus A320, A330 and A340. A European AST would be similarly equipped.

It may become practicable, by suction or other means, to remove the turbulent boundary layer from a wing surface and thus induce a laminar airflow. The nature and substance of the wing surface that would allow this, akin to the philosopher's stone in alchemy, does not, in the mid 1990s, exist. When it does, it will turn a base airflow into a golden one. On a subsonic wing at Mach 0.8, reducing the skin friction drag could reduce the overall drag by 45%, on Concorde at Mach 2, by 35%.

The Experimental Aircraft Programme (EAP) demonstrator aircraft for the European Fighter Aircraft (Tornado replacement) used electronic flying control systems. This allowed the pilot to retain control when the centre of gravity was so far to the rear as to make the aircraft unflyable without autostabilisation through 'Active controls'. An AST would rely heavily on this kind of technology. Other aspects like the canard and leading edge devices to the double delta planform are also relevant to an AST

The Rolls-Royce RB211 engine. The by-pass flow exits around the engine core. The frontal area, evident by the size of the by-pass duct, would cause too much drag at supersonic speeds and the jet velocity would be too low to give effective propulsion

At higher Mach numbers the reduction is not so great: Mach 3, 20% and Mach 4 only 8%. Incidentally a laminar flow would also subdue the shock wave.

With no turbulent mixing, the maximum temperature of the structure at places other than the leading edge is dramatically reduced. On Concorde at the wing root near the trailing edge this reduction would be from 113°C to 51°C; on the Blackbird (SR-71) at Mach 4, the drop is estimated to be from 257°C to 104°C, but with the loading edge at 547°C. An aluminium alloy is quite comfortable at 104°C. An AST cruising at Mach 3 might after all be possible. However, the apparatus capable of sustaining laminar flow would add some weight and complexity to the wing of the resulting aircraft.

If that apparatus turned out to be nothing more than cryogenic fuel, then the design of the AST might be radically altered. Liquid hydrogen or methane could, by virtue of cooling the wing surface, diminish the boundary layer, thus laminarising the air-flow.

Liquid hydrogen has good calorific value per kilogram but bad per litre; its exhaust contains water, no carbon dioxide and, depending on the design of the combustion chamber, only traces of oxides of nitrogen (NO_x). However, it is not energy efficient to extract it from fossil fuels.

Concorde's four Rolls-Royce kerosene burning Olympus engines represent the pinnacle of turbojet development. They each have an intake system whose area constantly changes during supersonic flight according to ambient conditions and

engine demand, which then leads into the engines themselves followed by the re-heat system upstream of two variable nozzles. Must the successor engine achieve more and can it be made to do so? The answer is of course yes to both questions.

Although Concorde's engines are highly efficient at supersonic speeds, they are inefficient and noisy at low speeds. Compounded by the high drag, the rate of fuel usage at the terminal area manoeuvring speed of 250 kts is 50 kgs per mile. On final approach at 160 kts this increases to 150 kgs per mile. This compares with 15 kgs per mile used during the latter portion of the supersonic cruise.

Even if noise suppressors worked, they do not improve engine efficiency at low speed. The best choice for the AST would seem to be an engine with a variable cycle. This would reduce noise and the off-design fuel burn. For take-off, subsonic flight and landing, the new engine must be able to perform like a high by-pass engine (with high mass flow of air, but with low jet exhaust velocity), as on a Boeing 747. Then for supersonic flight, the engine would transform itself into a turbojet (with a low mass of air flow but with high jet exhaust velocity), as per Concorde. All this while it maintains the lowest specific fuel consumption possible.

Rolls-Royce and SNECMA (the Concorde powerplant partners) having pooled their ideas, are, in the mid 1990s, proposing a 'Mid Tandem Fan' engine for the AST. On take-off each engine would receive air from two intakes, the normal front intake leading to the first stages of the compressor, and side intakes with 'blow in' doors, to feed a mid fan turning on the same shaft. The mid

An HS 125 with the left-hand Rolls-Royce Viper turbo-jet modified to test various engine silencer designs

One of the configurations tested during investigations into engine silencing by Rolls-Royce and McDonnell Douglas

fan flow would by-pass the engine core, before surrounding the core exhaust flow and then exiting via the secondary nozzle. The amount of energy delivered to the low pressure spool (turning front compressors and the mid fan) would depend on the area of the primary nozzle (see diagram) – the greater the area the higher the by-pass flow.

After take-off the by-pass ratio will decrease (from about two to one) causing the jet velocity to increase as the Mach number increases. The jet velocity on take-off must not exceed 450 metres per second (Mach 1 = 340 m/s), otherwise the noise regulations (FAR part 36 Stage 3) will be infringed. The high by-pass (therefore quieter) engines, introduced in the 1970s, outlawed the preceding generation of noisier airliners and embarrassed Concorde's supporters. The AST is unlikely to meet a similar situation, as any future fan engines will exhibit only a small, but not revolutionary, noise reduction. Provided the noise rules governing the AST are established at the outset and achieved at the finish, all will be well.

The payload to weight ratio on Concorde is barely 6%. A subsonic airliner over a similar range (3,300 nm) can achieve 15%. For each passenger on Concorde there is about 1¾ tonnes of aircraft (and fuel) – on a B747 the figure is less than a tonne. Each passenger on Concorde accounts for just less than a tonne of fuel in crossing the Atlantic (17 passenger statute miles per gallon), whilst a Boeing 747 betters this by a factor of three and the smaller 767 by over four.

According to a Boeing study, high temperature thermoplastic or polyimide polymeric composites for speeds less than Mach

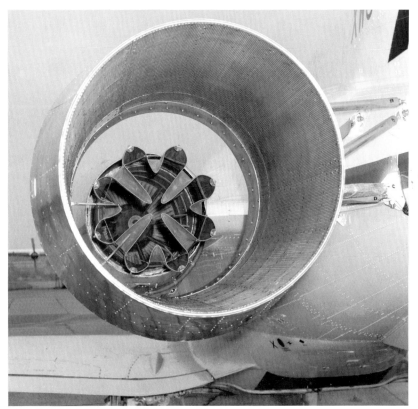

2.8 will be able to replace some of the alloy structures of the 1960s. Where metal is essential, techniques like the plastic forming and diffusion bonding of, for instance, Titanium can be employed to build matrices. Both methods reduce the structural mass. To repeat, on Concorde it costs a ton of fuel to carry an extra ton. Such structural techniques reduce the mass, therefore the thrust requirement, therefore the engine size, thus the fuel burn and thus the take-off weight. By 1990 an AST of similar range and payload to Concorde would have weighed 125 tonnes, compared to Concorde's 185.

The AST must have an engine that can 'change gear'. It will then be able to cope with low speeds like the big fan engine on the B747's wing on the right, and for supersonic cruise like the Rolls-Royce Olympus engine as seen on Concorde taxying here to the British Airways terminal at New York's JFK International. The Rolls-Royce Mid Tandem Fan proposal could fulfil this exacting role

Turning now to the question of pollution from engine exhaust gases, oxides of nitrogen (NO_x) are formed when the combustion is close to stoichiometric – from the endothermic combination of atmospheric nitrogen and oxygen. There is a NO_x emission index, and it is a measure of the pollutant produced per unit of fuel burnt. On Concorde it is 19. A figure of 5 is both desirable and attainable without impairing the efficiency of a future engine, thanks to modifications carried out on the combustion chamber. One Pratt and Whitney proposal arranges the combustion to be rich, followed by a 'quick quench'.

Chloro-fluoro-carbons (CFCs) from aerosols, fire extinguishers and refrigerants, probably threaten the ozone layer more than the NO_x emitted in aircraft exhaust. NO_x possibly even destroys CFCs. The ozone layer is found between 30,000 and 150,000 ft above the earth's surface. Ozone (triatomic oxygen – O_3) filters out some of the ultra violet light which, in excess, can cause skin cancer. In the stratosphere above the tropopause (37,000 ft), less atmospheric mixing occurs. The higher the molecule

finds itself the longer it remains. One 'rogue' molecule can, by catalytic action, be responsible for the destruction of many ozone molecules. The wind blows even in the stratosphere, with the resultant mixing cleaning it out more quickly than was originally predicted.

Volcanoes are another source of pollution. During its eruption in June 1991, Mount Pinatubo (in the Philippines) hurled tons of pollutants into the atmosphere. Just prior to eruption, sulphur dioxide (a source of acid rain), was being emitted at the rate of 5000 tons per day. On eruption, a volume of 5-8 cubic kilometres of ash were spewed forth, some of which attained an altitude of over 100,000 ft. It has been estimated that debris in the atmosphere from this eruption alone will have caused global temperatures to have been depressed by over 1°C for up to five years. In calculating what level of pollution would be caused by a fleet of 1000 ASTs, all other possible sources should be examined and compared.

Even if NO_x generated by aeroengines is not a major threat to the ozone layer, it must, if possible, be suppressed. This, not least from the political point of view, caused Concorde's entry into the States to be delayed in 1976 while accusations, many of them false, of its committing environmental sins were being investigated.

Boeing is investigating a modified aerodynamic design which promises, at about Mach 1.7, some alleviation from the sonic boom by rounding off of the N wave (see page 60). By reducing the rate of rise of the overpressure, the startle effect of the bang is diminished. If so it might become acceptable to fly at reduced supersonic speeds over 'boom sensitive' land. At about M 1.2, the shock wave is usually refracted away from the surface, thanks to the temperature differential between the aircraft's altitude and the surface. This effect is greater when there is a headwind at the aircraft's altitude compared to that on the surface; the other way round and the effect is reversed. But cruise Mach numbers less than about M 1.4 are inefficient, as the L/D is reduced without the compensating precompression effect in the intakes giving superior efficiency to the engines.

The propagation, by Concorde, of secondary shock waves (see page 58) caused some complaints from the ground. A modified track, or an earlier deceleration, alleviates the problem. That very low secondary disturbances are noticeable does suggest that any kind of primary boom over populated land may not be tolerable.

The only real option for the AST is to have sufficient range to avoid a surface sensitive to the sonic boom and, where this is not possible, to be as fuel efficient at Mach 0.95 as at Mach 2. Consider flying from London to Tokyo at Mach 2. The great circle (shortest) track via Scandinavia and eastern Russia (CIS) is 5173 nm (5¼ hrs). Avoiding Scandinavia, but using a supersonic corridor between Lena and Okhotsk, the distance becomes 5550 nm (5½ hrs). Finally, avoiding all land, flying south west from the Bering Strait to Tokyo, 6311 nm (6¼ hrs). Cruising in at Mach 0.85 via the great circle route, it takes about 11 hours.

Many of the 1990s studies propose an

 Mid tandem fan supersonic propulsion system

Auxiliary intakes at take-off

Auxiliary intakes at cruise

The Mid-Tandem-Fan engine proposal by Rolls-Royce and SNECMA, with an ultra-low emissions combustor and no re-heat. For noise suppression and efficiency throughout the speed range, an engine whose by-pass ratio can be varied is virtually essential for the AST. An extra fan is placed around the 'waist' of the engine (in order to reduce frontal area) and driven by the same shaft that drives the low pressure compressor. High by-pass flow, for low forward speed, is achieved by opening the primary nozzle and arranging the fan inlet guide vanes for maximum flow; low by-pass, for supersonic cruise, by reducing primary nozzle area and adjusting the guide vanes for minimum flow

To accommodate the extra by-pass flow with low forward speed, extra 'blow-in' auxiliary intakes would be required. In this way the frontal area of the engine, vital for low drag, can be kept to a minimum

Left
One of the legacies of the B2707 was development of the 'glass cockpit' – the replacement of conventional electro-mechanical instruments with computer-generated depictions of instruments and aircraft situation. Here on a Boeing 757 the 'artificial horizon' looks like its mechanical predecessor, but the 'compass' can be made to show the predicted position of the aircraft, vertical and horizontal, as well as the actual. Accurate flying saves time and fuel – very apposite for an AST

Far left
18 May 1986. Concorde in formation with two Spitfires over Biggin Hill, which was an appropriate reunion as it was a Photo Reconnaissance Spitfire that paved the way to supersonic flight in 1943 (The Spitfire Society)

Bottom left
Dawn Colorado Springs, midday London, 5 November 1985, prior to the return of the Concorde charter flight via New York

AST with about 300 seats, with a maximum take-off weight of about 300 tonnes. This would improve the payload to weight ratio from Concorde's 6% to about 10% over a range of 5500 nautical miles (nm) – roughly 2000 nm more than Concorde.

There is, however, a proposal from Lockheed for a 100 seater 100 tonne supersonic transport of similar range. Although its engines are not of the variable cycle type (see above) it is said that it will be able to meet the FAR 36 Stage 3 noise rules. Lockheed, although not chosen for the original US SST project, have had considerable supersonic experience notably with the SR-71 Blackbird which was capable of speeds well in excess of Mach 3.

A 1990 proposal for a supersonic business jet by Gulfstream (USA) with Sukhoi of the then Soviet Union and Rolls-Royce of UK, seems, by 1994, to have been shelved. For low supersonic drag an aircraft must have a high fineness ratio (length to maximum diameter) – hence Concorde's four abreast seating arrangement. On an aircraft with a short fuselage the internal volume (for fuel and passengers) is therefore compromised. The operating costs of the AST might well exceed those of a subsonic airliner. The market would need to determine what level of surcharge would be acceptable in view of the time saved.

Mid 1990 studies suggest that a three class aircraft with a 15% surcharge over existing subsonic fares would be acceptable. Some caution must be registered here, however. Concorde was barely competitive price-wise when compared to the subsonic jets of the 1960s. Thus Concorde's delayed entry into service during the economic recession of 1976, and well after the debut of the highly economic Boeing 747, compounded its already difficult marketing position. The AST must not be compromised in a similar way.

Most studies favour a cruising speed of between Mach 1.7 and Mach 2.4. Higher speeds do not proportionally reduce flight times, as a substantial part of the flight must be spent in acceleration and deceleration. However without laminar flow control, higher speeds add disproportionately to the difficulties. These mount as the temperature associated with the higher Mach numbers is reached. Not only must the

materials and structure become more sophisticated, but also the fluids – fuel, oil and hydraulic. Stagnation temperature at Mach 1.7 in ISA (International Standard Atmosphere) conditions is 68°C, Mach 2, 116°C, at Mach 2.4, 192°C and at Mach 3 it is 332°C (see appendix for formula).

There is an alternative to the AST described above. That is to wait, perhaps over 50 years, for a derivative of the space launch vehicle that could have been developed by the mid 21st century. This is the subject of the final chapter.

Opposite
Avion de Grande Vitesse – a hypersonic proposal from Aerospatiale. Not exo-atmospheric, the AGV would still generate a sonic boom, experience high skin temperatures and be very expensive to develop. Evolving a Mach 2 successor built on the experience gained from Concorde could be preferable

Opposite below
A fitting descendant to Concorde in name – Alliance – implying continuing technological collaboration, could be this Aerospatiale proposals for un Avion de Transport Supersonique Futur (ATSF). Cruising with 200 passengers over 6500 nm between Mach 2 and 2.5, it would be propelled by variable cycle engines

Below
British Airways confidence and pride in its flag carrier Concorde is exemplified by the multi-million pound refurbishment programme instituted in 1993. The picture illustrates the third example of Concorde's cabin furnishings since entry into service in 1976

Sub-Orbital Travel

At a speed of 15,000 kts (Mach 26 in the atmosphere), an object would be capable of orbiting the earth. Providing there was no aerodynamic drag it would require no thrust and, being weightless (but not massless), no lift. Until sometime during the next century vehicles will need several stages to achieve Low Earth Orbit (LEO – 300 kms). Even the US Space Shuttle is assisted by two solid fuelled rocket boosters. These are refurbishable, unlike its vast external fuel tank which is sacrificed on every launch. To fractionalise the cost of placing a payload into LEO a vehicle must be developed that is capable of Single Stage To Orbit (SSTO) and return, in its entirety.

A variation of such a vehicle could 'fly' from London to Australia in about an hour. During the early 1980s in America, President Reagan announced, after a particularly tiring trip to the Far East, that something quicker than a Jumbo jet should be developed. Hence the US NASP (National Aero Space Plane) project, dubbed, thanks to the President, 'The Orient Express' – this, in spite of it being supposedly an orbital vehicle. The contender for SSTO on the other side of the Atlantic, but not conceived by a jet-lagged British head of state, was HOTOL.

A rocket using oxygen and hydrogen must carry these in a mass ratio of six to one – the burn is slightly rich. So, to avoid weighing the vehicle down with oxygen, it would be better to collect it from the atmosphere during the flight into orbit. On NASP a SCRamJet (Supersonic Combustion Ram Jet) is being investigated, in the hope of it eventually being able to thrust a 'demonstrator' into LEO.

Air compressed in an intake heats up. By avoiding the need to decelerate the air to subsonic speed during hypersonic flight (Mach 5+), the temperature rise can be contained. This allows a greater margin for adding heat during combustion. However, NASP has encountered problems and, in 1994, is on 'hold' at the time of writing. First, NASP needs an engine (turbojet or rocket) for take-off – ram jets cannot operate from rest. Secondly, above Mach 15 it requires a rocket, otherwise the intake would have become huge and the exhaust

The launch trolley (possibly rocket propelled) proposal for the air-breathing HOTOL would have to be capable of stopping its 250t payload in the event of an aborted take-off

University of Southampton

5.5 METRE WIND TUNNEL WARTON

View of a HOTOL scale model at Mach 8 being studied in a wind tunnel at Southampton University. A passenger on a suborbital flight would experience 30 minutes of acceleration, a short period of weightlessness (but not masslessness), followed by 30 minutes of deceleration. Total flight time from London to Sydney would be about 70 minutes! (Southampton University)

HOTOL would rely on separated airflow for lift at low speeds, seen here in a wind tunnel test with engine intake closed. As with the US Space Shuttle, it would land from a glide approach, with no ability to 'go-around'

temperature excessive. Thirdly, to operate in accelerating flight, internal variable geometry is required – expensive. Fourthly, for ideal combustion the necessarily very smooth airflow must, at the combustion point, be made suddenly turbulent to ensure mixing with the hydrogen – conflicting requirements. One engineer has dubbed NASP as 'the Smithsonian in orbit' (Aeronautical Museum in Washington). An alternative solution is to design a rocket engine which can first use atmospheric oxygen then, for Mach 5+, onboard liquid oxygen combusted with hydrogen fuel.

The RB545, whose patent was acquired by Rolls-Royce from its inventor Alan Bond, is such an engine and was designed for the British HOTOL (HOrizontal Take-Off and Landing). For take-off, from a rocket-propelled trolley, and initial wing borne climb, the engine 'breathes' air. Air, compressed in the intake, is cooled by a heat exchanger through which liquid hydrogen fuel is circulating. Then two-thirds of the hydrogen, before being dumped, drives a turbine to compress the air further, prior to combustion with the remaining one-third of the hydrogen in the rocket chambers.

By Mach 6, momentum drag in the intake about equals the thrust, excessive energy then being needed to remove heat at the exchanger and the speed becomes too great for an intake of practical size. Therefore nine minutes after take-off at 85,000 ft and Mach 5, the engine would be switched to rocket mode, using liquid oxygen. This would continue until the craft reaches a speed of 15,350 kts at an altitude of 300,000 ft. It would then coast under its

own momentum into LEO, at nearly 1,000,000 ft (300 kms) above the earth's surface.

The HOTOL design suffered from one major aerodynamic defect. Although the centre of lift moves rearwards during transonic acceleration it moves forward again at the higher Mach numbers. Excessive quantities of hydraulic power would have been necessary to apply a compensating 'down' aerodynamic force – this despite maximum movement of the centre of gravity.

The engine cycle of the RB545 is more intricate than described above and would have been expensive to develop. Private money might have been forthcoming, but Rolls-Royce was not prepared to go ahead with anything less than British Government involvement. As a result a rocket-propelled 'interim' HOTOL was proposed, to be launched at 30,000 ft from the back of the six-engined Russian transport aircraft, the Antonov An-225. British Aerospace was still involved in 1994.

In 1991, Alan Bond, unable to hawk his original idea around foreign financiers (it was then an Official Secret), invented another engine – SABRE. This is not patented, and thus not liable to be constrained by the Official Secrets Act.

SABRE stands for the Synergetic Air Breathing and Rocket Engine. Two such engines are proposed on Alan Bond's SKY-LON, which is a refined version of HOTOL. SKYLON could become the choice of FES-TIP (Future European Space Transportation Investigations Programme), and might, by 2005, be carrying 12 ton payloads (cf 7 tons on HOTOL, 28 tons on Shuttle) into LEO. It is estimated that the cost per launch could be as little as $(US)10.7. The Space Shuttle's recurring costs per launch are $615m, but are of course much more if the development cost is included.

During late 1993 configuration C1 of SKYLON was under consideration. Weighing 275 tonnes it would take-off towards the east from an equatorial runway (to gain maximum benefit from the earth's spin) using its own undercarriage. It has the ability to reject take-off. Having covered 2.8 kms during a 36 second $\frac{1}{2}$g acceleration to 'rotate' speed (about 350 mph, Mach 0.5), SKYLON would become airborne. In airbreathing mode the total thrust would be 220 tons. SKYLON would then switch to rocket mode (300 tons thrust) in a similar manner to HOTOL, for transition into LEO.

The configuration of SKYLON allows for better centre of gravity control than was possible with HOTOL. Centrally mounted wings and engines allow usage of liquid hydrogen fuel from tanks at the fore and aft extremities of the fuselage. Pitch control would be enhanced with a canard surface, whereas the fin, in configuration C1, is placed aft.

After a $1m kick off fee, SKYLON would need investment from public funds. Alan Bond was hoping that $200m would be forthcoming as a government high risk investment, repayable if SKYLON worked. Once the concept had been proved, some

kind of Venture Capital would be sought. Bearing in mind the financial lessons from the Concorde project, Bond insists that: 1) a truthful initial estimate of the cost of SKYLON should be submitted, no matter how great; 2) the size of SKYLON should be established before starting; so that 3) only one version of SKYLON is built, not three as in the case of Concorde. The first flight into orbit should be within seven years of the start of the project, with return on investment within ten. This reflects the theory that longer time scales are financially unattractive. However, in May 1994 further cuts in Britain's space budget made the choice of SKYLON to fulfil the FESTIP requirement appear unlikely.

That the next step in aerospace engineering is being proposed and researched by a few dedicated enthusiasts, and not by a multi-national company, says volumes about human innovation. The Wright brothers, von Braun and Sir Frank Whittle are examples of independent innovators. The great multi-national companies, with so much to lose if things go wrong, are possibly not the ideal oysters in which to attempt to culture revolutionary pearls. Nevertheless, they have a vital part to play once theory has become practice. Just when it seemed that space exploration had to be dominated by the great battalions, the home computer, itself spawned by the space age, became powerful enough to allow one individual to replace the ranks of draughtsmen without whom, it must be

Orbiter -0068
23.V.91

Deployable Foreplanes

LOx Tanks

LH₂ Tank

Payload Bay

Interim HOTOL. Drag at low altitude being of less consideration, this version is more bulbous than air breathing HOTOL. Other studies have placed the fin at the rear

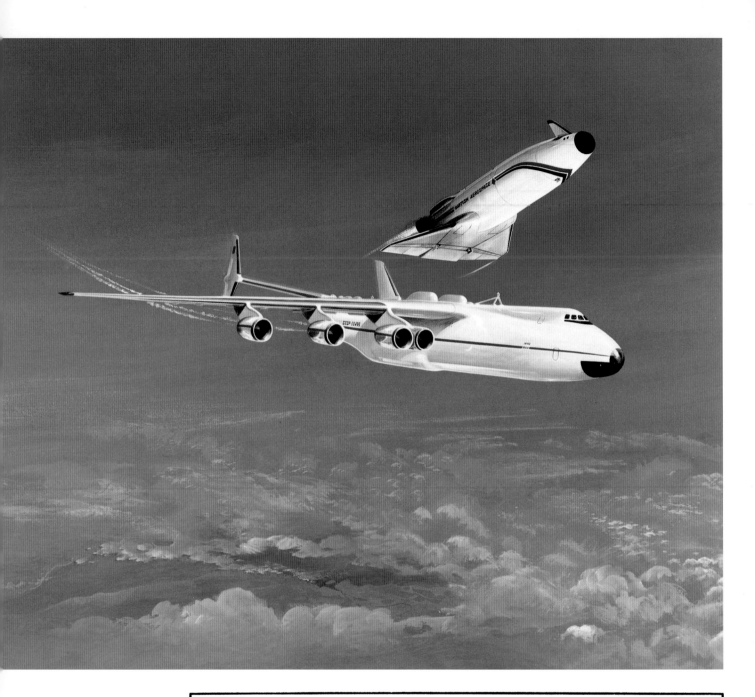

The launch technique from the An-225 would require a pull up to give HOTOL lift for separation, followed immediately by a dive to avoid the flame plumes from the orbiter's four pure rocket engines (total thrust about 200,000 lbs). Only from a surface launched airbreathing derivative of HOTOL could there be evolved an economic sub-orbital transport

T+4 sec h = 9.2 km
Main Engine Ignition

T = 0 sec h = 9.2 km
Orbiter Separates

T-10 min h = 9.4 km
Turn onto heading
Set up launch

T-62 sec h = 9.4 km
Begin powered dive

T-15 sec h = 8.8 km
Pull up for Separation

T > 4 sec h = 9.1 km
An-225 Separation
Manoeuvre

Left
The rocket-powered 'Interim' HOTOL proposal, being launched at Mach 0.8 from 31,000 ft off the back of the giant Russian An-225 – capable of lifting a 250t HOTOL complete with 7t payload – shown here with eight engines. In 1990, with lack of funds to develop the RB545 hybrid (capable of using either atmospheric or liquid oxygen) engine, BAe began exploring this way of providing a cheap satellite launch system for Europe

The US National Aerospace Plane (NASP), or X-30, proposal. During the 1960s, rocket propelled X-15s attained 354,000 ft and Mach 6.7. However, the programme was cancelled before a ramjet propelled version could be fully tested. In the 1980s, under the auspices of NASA, a team of several contractors was formed to research and develop a craft capable of 'Single Stage To Orbit'. The main thruster of NASP should be the Supersonic Combustion Ram Jet. However, to work it must have sufficient forward speed, say Mach 1+, then from Mach 15 up to Mach 25 (necessary for orbital flight) there is little room to add heat to the super heated intake flow. Furthermore, the huge intake (itself a major structural headache) required at Mach 15 makes slower flight extremely inefficient

SKYLON (after a similarly named and looking structure at the 1951 'Festival of Britain') – an evolution of the HOTOL concept. Propulsion would be by two pairs of four SABRE hybrid engines. It is designed to be capable of take-off from its own undercarriage, flight into Low Earth Orbit and return without shedding any rocket assisted stages. The movement of centre of gravity, through propellant usage, to compensate for the variation of centre of pressure with speed, is not compromised by a rear-mounted engine

The Two Stage to Orbit (TSTO) proposal from Aerospatiale

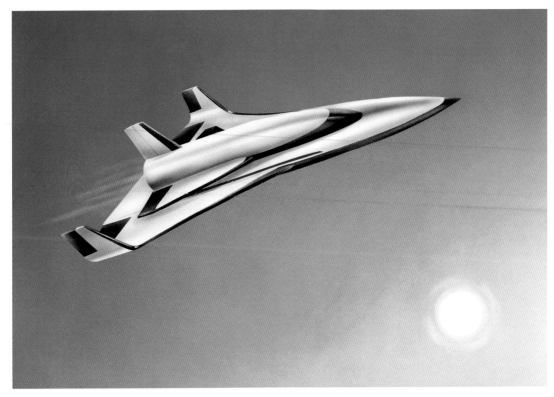

Aerospatiale's version of a Single Stage to Orbit (SSTO) vehicle would be propelled by a turbo-rocket-ramjet unit

admitted, there would have been neither Concorde, nor a manned trip to the moon.

The French and German proposals for the next generation of space launch vehicles are (like NASP) still the children of the great companies. However, they envisage two stages. The first, a hypersonic air-breathing vehicle from which the second stage, a rocket propelled orbiter, would be launched, with both stages being reusable. It would be from the first stage that a hypersonic transporter could be developed.

Incidentally, the German proposal derives its name from an engineer called Sänger. While working during World War 2, he designed a vehicle that, launched from Germany, would bounce along the upper atmosphere, bomb New York, complete the earth orbit then return to Germany. It was not built.

If resources for aerospace projects are finite, what kind of project most merits investment? The Ultra High Capacity Transport (UHCT) to replace the Jumbo, a reusable SSTO vehicle or the AST? Airports would need radical alterations to accommodate a 600 tonne UHCT, modified buildings, wider taxyways and greater runway strengths. Perhaps the distance between landing UHCTs and smaller aircraft would have to be increased to allow time for the powerful vortices to dissipate, thus reducing the number of landings per hour. An SSTO would open up the infinite resource of space, but at some economic risk. Almost as risky is the AST. But the latter two are infinitely more exciting, and people do pay for excitement. Space tourism – a week in orbit – may become an economic reality.

Should major projects be collaborative? World-wide collaboration has the advantage of ensuring universal acceptance, a well spread risk and the building of fewer versions. Competition, on the other hand, is a great spur. Without the Soviets taking an early lead in space, it is doubtful whether the US would have gone to the moon so quickly. In the 1960s, Europe wanted to retrieve her pre-eminent place in aviation – hence, among other things, Concorde.

Without the competitive element two things happen: the proposal to build can be more dispassionately analysed, but the urgency to start diminishes. However, as soon as it appears that an AST and/or

space plane will have attractive economic prospects, then the building of only one collaborative version will become inevitable.

Man is by nature an innovator. Technology is his plaything and economics the measure of his efforts. What is inevitable is that the next aerospace projects will still need men of the stature of Sir George Edwards and André Puget, the former's opposite number in Sud Aviation, to guide them to fruition.

In 1992 Robert McKinlay, former Concorde engineer and Chairman of British Aerospace Airbus Ltd said, in a lecture entitled *Concorde First or Last*: 'In the year 2010 grandfathers are not going to want to say to their grandchildren, "We used to cross the Atlantic in three and a half hours".'

A 1990s concept for space transportation – Sänger. Here, at 115,000 ft and Mach 6.8, the rocket-propelled orbiter 'Horus' is seen separating from the hypersonic ascent stage propelled, in one study, by a concentrically arranged turbo ramjet engine. Above Mach 3.5 only the ramjet would be in operation. A commercial hypersonic vehicle might be developed from this. 'Sänger' is named after the World War 2 engineer who proposed bombing America from Germany. Once launched, his craft would have bounced in and out of the atmosphere, released its load over New York, completed its earth orbit with diminishing skips, and finally glided back to Germany

Powerful computers and complex algorithms have revolutionised design. By 1845 the Navier-Stokes equations for the computation of fluid dynamics had been formulated. They remained virtually insoluble until the era of the supercomputer over 100 years later. Here, a temperature plot of the hypersonic Sänger/Horus combination is shown

Appendices

Max take-off weight	185,070 kg (408,000 lb)
Max landing weight	111,130 kg (245,000 lb)
Max weight without fuel	92,080 kg (203,000 lb)
Max payload (approx)	13,150 kg (29,000 lb)
Max number of passengers	128 (but BA Concordes are fitted with 100 passenger seats)
Max fuel at specific gravity 0,800 limited by volume:	95,680 kg (26,400) gallons)

The dimensions of Concorde. The measurement marked with the asterisk is for the 'Aerodynamic Root Reference Chord'. It is used when referring to the position of the centre of gravity moved by the transference of fuel (see accompanying diagram). Thus the centre of gravity on most take-offs (53.5%) is 48 ft 6 in behind the forward point, and 53 ft 6 in at its most rearward (59%) during the supersonic cruise.

Concorde – Leading dimensions

Breguet Range Equation

The maximum range is constrained by several factors including payload, reserve fuel required on arrival, weather conditions and the amount of the route that can be flown supersonically. A typical maximum range on Concorde with 100 passengers plus baggage (10,000 kg total payload) and normal fuel reserves, is 3,500 nm (4,030 sm). The route between Bahrain and Singapore was flown in the colder air found over the tropics; this improved the efficiency of the engines allowing a range of 3,720 nm to be flown regularly. Although the payload limit on this sector was 7,500 kg (75 passengers) it could usually be increased to close on 100 passengers when conditions were favourable. The maximum recorded range on Concorde under very favourable conditions, and therefore difficult to plan in advance, was between Washington and Nice, a distance of 3,965 nm (4,565 sm) flown on 11 September 1984 with 54 passengers in G-BOAB taking 4 hours and 7 minutes.

The range (R) in nautical miles (no wind) of an aircraft can be expressed as:

$$R = \frac{V \times L/D}{SFC} \times \log_e (w_1/w_2)$$

Where V is the cruising speed in knots; L/D the lift to drag ratio; SFC is the specific fuel consumption of the engine – pounds of fuel per hour per pound of engine thrust; (w_1/w_2) is the ratio of weights at the start and end of the sample of range to be investigated. The natural logarithm of the final term is a measure of the structural efficiency of the aircraft – the amount of fuel available for aircraft weight (including payload). For Concorde travelling at Mach 2, V is circa 1120 kts; L/D is 7.5; SFC 1.18 (each engine consuming fuel at just over 11,000 lbs per hour will give, during the cruise, about 9300 lbs of thrust). If the two weights were 165 and 110 tonnes respectively, Concorde could travel just under 2900 nautical miles on 55 tonnes of fuel. Should the weights have been 155 t and 100 t respectively, then the range improves to 3120 nms. In practice over 90 tonnes of fuel is loaded including approximately 15 tonnes of 'spare' fuel for diversion etc, and much of the fuel is burnt during the 'off design' period of the flight. However, the equation can be applied to each segment of the flight.

Powerplant

Four Rolls-Royce/SNECMA Olympus 593 Mark 610 turbo jet engines. Maximum thrust at take-off with afterburner (reheat) contributing about 20% to the total – 38,050 lb.

At take-off 95% of the thrust is delivered by the engine and 5% by the nozzle and intake assemblies.

During supersonic cruise only 50% of the thrust is delivered by the engine; the remainder is delivered, equally shared, by the variable ramp assembly and the convergent/divergent nozzle system. The purpose of the diffuser is to slow, and therefore compress, the air, which is now subsonic, still further before it enters the engine face.

Note *A convergent passage slows and compresses a supersonic airflow, while a divergent passage slows and compresses a subsonic airflow.*

Above *The Olympus engine is a two-spool engine. The inner, or low pressure (1p) shaft revolves within the outer, or high pressure (hp) shaft. There are fourteen compressor stages, seven on each shaft, driven by their respective turbines. As the air approaches the combustion chambers, during the supersonic cruise, it becomes very hot due to its compression (over 80:1 total). hence the need to construct the final four compression stages from a nickel-based alloy – usually reserved for the turbine area. (The darker shades, green in the cutaway engine below, show the more heat resistant alloys.) To the rear of the turbines is the reheat assembly. The amount of fuel burnt in the combustion chamber controls the rpm of the hp shaft, whilst varying the area of the primary nozzle (see top) controls, at a given rpm of the hp shaft, the rpm of the 1p shaft.*

The anatomy of Concorde

Fuel

F1 Forward trim tanks (nos 9 and 10)
F2 Forward collector tank (nos 1 and 4)
F3 Aft collector tanks (nos 2 and 3)
F4 Aft trim tank (no 11)
F5 Fuel jettison
F6 Tank vent gallery
F7 Tank overflow and pressure-relief lines (normal venting at F23)
F8 Inlet (to tank) control valve
F9 Contents unit
F10 Transfer pumps (nos 5A and 7A tanks) in fairing
F11 Engine-feed system
F12 Accumulator
F13 Trim transfer gallery (and refuel and jettison)
F14 Engine-feed pumps
F15 Transfer pumps
F16 Air-cooled tank walls
F17 Dry bay over engines
F18 Tank end walls
F19 Fuel/hydraulic oil heat exchanger
F20 Fuel tank (no 8)
F21 Fuel tank (no 6)
F22 Vent and pressurisation system
F23 Normal venting orifice

Powerplant

P1 Rolls-Royce Bristol/Snecma Olympus 593 of 38,050 lb thrust with reheat
P2 Nacelle suspension links
P3 Honeycomb intake-nose section
P4 Boundary-layer splitter
P5 Boundary-layer separation wall
P6 Intake front ramp
P7 Intake rear ramp
P8 Ramp-control hydraulic motors, gearbox and screw-jacks
P9 Dump-door actuators and linkage
P10 Spill door
P11 Access panel
P12 Inlet flap
P13 Ramp spill air to lower fire doors
P14 Fire flaps
P15 Nacelle to wing mounting beam
P16 Engine front support link
P17 Engine main mounting (pin-jointed to wing)
P18 Engine thrust struts
P19 Engine-mounting transverse equaliser
P20 Aft nacelle support link
P21 Heat shield (stainless steel/refractory material sandwich)
P22 Aft nacelle sidewall and nozzle-support structure
P23 Afterburner ring
P24 Primary variable nozzle
P25 Nozzle-mounting spigots
P26 Pneumatic nozzle-actuator
P27 Combined secondary nozzle and reverser buckets
P28 Bucket-actuating screw-jacks
P29 Air motor
P30 Non-structural engine-access doors
P31 Oil tank

Radio and electronics

R1 Radio and electronics racking
R2 Circuit-breaker panels
R3 Electrics bay
R4 Aft electronics bay (port and stbd)
R5 VHF 1 antenna
R6 HF slot antenna
R7 VOR antenna
R8 Electrics connectors
R9 Electric conduits
R10 Weather radar

Undercarriage

U1 Machined nose-gear mounting beams
U2 Nose-gear hinge
U3 Side braces
U4 Retraction jack (free-fall emergency lowering)
U5 Telescopic drag strut
U6 Rack and pinion steering motors ± 60°
U7 Nosewheel tyres: 31 in × 10.75 – 14 in. 175 lb/sq in
U8 Mainwheel tyres: 47 in × 15.75 – 22 in, 187 lb/sq in
U9 Provision in wheels for fan-cooling of brakes (upper wheel omitted for clarity)
U10 Bogie beam damper
U11 Pre-shortening mechanism
U12 Tail bumper, retractable (twin 3.26 × 120 – 4.5 in wheels (294 lb/sq in)
U13 Shock absorber
U14 Retraction jack

FLIGHT INTERNATIONAL

F. MUNGER

The Flight Envelope

How the fuel is used to move the centre of gravity on Concorde. The position of the centre of gravity is measured as a percentage of the 'Aerodynamic Root Reference Chord' (see dimension chart). The position of the centre of gravity restricts the aircraft to a speed range shown by the 'limit bugs' on the Machmeter; or alternatively, at a given speed, the centre of gravity must be within limits shown by 'bugs' on the centre of gravity indicator (see photographs on pages 89, 92 and 100)

Concorde must be flown within the slightly shaded area shown on the graph. The maximum operating indicated airspeed limit (V_{MO}) varies not only with altitude, but also, to a small extent, with Concorde's weight. Above 51,000 ft the maximum operating Mach limit (M_{MO}) over-rules V_{MO}; by 60,000 ft M_{MO} (Mach 2.04) corresponds to 440 knots indicated airspeed. The lowest authorised speed limit below 15,000 ft is not shown on this graph since it is related either to weight on take-off from a particular runway, or to landing weight.

Although M_{MO} is Mach 2.04, Concorde generally cruises at Mach 2. There are, however, further constraints to the speed. One is derived from the position of the centre of gravity; at the furthest forward position of the centre of gravity, the top Mach number limit is Mach 0.8; during the acceleration the centre of gravity is moved progressively rearward and at its most rearward point the Mach number range is from Mach 1.55 to over Mach 2.04; however, the top speed is then limited by M_{MO}, V_{MO} or T_{MO}. T_{MO} is the maximum operating temperature limit, representing another constraint to the speed; the maximum temperature at the nose must not exceed 127°C.

In practice this does not become a limiting factor to Concorde until the outside air temperature is warmer than −50°C, at altitudes above 48,000 ft.

Next to the altitude, in thousands of feet, is shown the outside air temperature corresponding to the International Standard Atmosphere (ISA). Next to this is shown the speed of sound for that given temperature. The true outside air temperature is usually at variance from the 'standard' by a few degrees either way over the North Atlantic, so the figure for the speed of sound must be regarded as approximate. Over the equator, where the tropopause is higher, temperatures between 50,000 and 60,000 ft are of the order of ISA −20°C (i.e. −77°C). At this temperature the speed of sound is 545 knots (627 mph).

The formula for the speed of sound (a) is

$$a = \text{constant} \times \sqrt{\text{absolute temperature}}$$

assuming temperature in °K and speed in knots, the constant = 38.89

For an outside air temperature of −57°C (216°K)

$$a = 38.89 \times \sqrt{216}$$
$$= 571 \text{ knots}$$

The formula for giving the approximate rise in temperature (ΔT)°C for a given speed is

$$\Delta T = \left(\frac{\text{speed in mph}}{100} \right)^2$$

Thus at Mach 2 when the outside air temperature is −57°C the temperature rise is

$$\left(\frac{2 \times 657.5}{100} \right)^2$$
$$\simeq 173°C$$

Under these conditions the total temperature is 173° − 57° = 116°C.

Note At the speeds associated with a Space Shuttle (or HOTOL) re-entering the earth's atmosphere this formula is not applicable.

The Aircraft

Type	Registration	number	First flight	Retired, now at
Prototype	F-WTSS	001	March 69	Le Bourget
Prototype	G-BSST	002	April 69	Yeovilton
Pre-prod.	G-AXDN	01	Dec 71	Duxford
Pre-prod.	F-WTSA	02	Jan 73	Orly
Production	F-WTSB	201	Dec 73	Toulouse
Production	G-BBDG	202	Feb 74	Filton
Production	F-WTSC[1]	203	Jan 75	
Production	G-BOAC	204	Feb 75	
Production	F-BVFA	205	Oct 75	
Production	G-BOAA	206	Nov 75	
Production	F-BVFB	207	March 76	
Production	G-BOAB	208	May 76	
Production	F-BVFC	209	July 76	
Production	G-BOAD	210	August 76	
Production	F-BVFD	211	Feb 77	
Production	G-BOAE	212	March 77	
Production	F-WJAM[2]	213	June 78	
Production	G-BFKW[3]	214	April 78	
Production	F-WJAN[4]	215	Dec 78	
Production	G-BFKX[5]	216	April 79	

1 Later F-BTSC. 2 Later F-BTSD. 3 Later G-BOAG. 4 Later F-BVFF. 5 Later G-BOAF.

Concorde Utilisation Details for British Airways and Air France

BA figures end of January 1994

Aircraft registration	Aircraft no.	Hours flown	Supersonic* cycles	Landings
BOAA	206	17765	5303	6375
BOAB	208	16968	5046	6015
BOAC	204	16721	5037	5963
BOAD	210	17280	5131	6100
BOAE	212	17213	5118	6353
BOAF	216	12386	3863	4086
BOAG	214	10169	3204	3662
BA total:		108505	32702	38554

Air France figures end of January 1994

Aircraft registration	Aircraft no.	Hours flown	Supersonic* cycles	Landings
BVFA	205	13595	4171	5217
BVFB	207	12064	3712	4219
BVFC	209	10520	3243	3606
BVFD	211	5814	1807	1929
BVFF	215	8684	2680	2914
BTSC	203	8812	2754	3937
BTSD	213	9195	2814	3422
Air France total:		68689	21181	25244
Grand total		177193	53883	63798

British Airways Concorde Crews 1976-1993**

Captains	First Officers	Engineer Officers
R P W Allen	A B Atkinson	S L Bolton
K P Barton	R P Babbé	G S Bowden
R J L Boas	M Bannister	R C Bricknell
J A D Bradshaw	A J Bird	A A Brown
D A Brister	P Benson	W J Brown
N A Britton	S Bohill-Smith	A Chalmers
A L Budd	M E Boyle	P C Carrigan
J D Butterley	L D Brodie	T F Caster
J W Burton	R J S Burchell	M Cooper
B J Calvert	M W Burke	T B Dewis
J L Chorley	A D Cobley	W Dobbs
J D Cook	A R Darke	F W Duffy
R V Dixon	P M Douglas	R Eades
P R W Duffey	J Downey	P E Egginton
J D Eames	D A Edmondson	I R Fellowes-
D H Ellis	J Graham	Freeman
M Emmett	C D Green	S G Floyd
V Gunton	B Harmer	J Goatham
J A Harkness	A I Heald	M Harrison
T Henderson	B R Holland	W G Hornby
J W Hirst	J G Huson	D Hoyle
P W Horton	B Irven	W D Johnston
J C Hutchinson	D A MacDonald-Lawson	W A Johnstone
K D Leney	D G Mitchell	I V Kirby
H J Linfield	E E R Murton	J E Lidiard
W D Lowe	C E Norris	P A Ling
A J Massie	B R Oliver	D A Macdonald
C B McMahon	T Orchard	P J Newman
H C McMullen	C J D Orlebar	T Norcott
I C McNeilly	J H Phillingham	P J Phillips
A R Meadows	J Phillips	T J Quarrey
R A Mills	R Pike	J A Rodger
C J C Morley	W J Piper	I F Smith
C C Morris	A F Quartly	J Stanbridge
G F Mussett	N S Rendall	G Tullier
K Myers	J M Reynolds	R N Webb
D J M Rendall	C A Robey	N C West
E Reynolds	M L Robson	A F Winstanley
M A Riley	R A Routledge	R Woodcock
S Robertson	P T Sinclair	
M Robinson	W I Smith	
D G Ross	K Snell	
D C Rowland	R J Taylor	
R S Smith	M H J Watson	
B G T Titchener	M H Watson	
N V Todd	J R White	
B O Walpole	D Whitton	
S D Wand	K Williams	
	M R Withey	
	M R Young	
	A J Yule	

*The rig at Farnborough achieved 20,000 'equivalent' supersonic cycles. Before the total of supersonic flight cycles reaches one third of this total a review will take place. However there is no finite limit to the life of the airframe.

**This is a list of all the BA crew members that have ever been qualified to operate Concorde. In 1980 there was a maximum of 28 qualified crews, since then the average has been about 20. A 'crew' consists of Captain, First Officer and Engineer Officer.

Concorde chronology

1956
November 5: Supersonic Transport Aircraft Committee (STAC) established.

1959
March 9: STAC recommends design studies of two supersonic airliners (Mach 1.2 and Mach 2).

1959–61
French and British SST feasibility and design studies initiated.

1961
First Anglo-French discussions on possible SST collaboration. *June–July*: First BAC/Sud discussions in Paris and Weybridge.

1962
October: Anglo-French Mach 2.2 transport specification published. *November 29*: Anglo-French agreement for joint design development and manufacture of a supersonic airliner.

1963
Preliminary design presented to airlines. *January 13*: President de Gaulle uses name 'Concorde'. *June 3*: Concorde sales option signed by Pan American Airlines. *June*: BOAC and Air France sign Concorde sales options. *June 5*: US supersonic transport programme announced.

1964
Projected medium-range version abandoned; design of long-range version enlarged. *May*: Enlarged Concorde design announced. *July*: Olympus 593D first run, Bristol.

1965
April: Metal cut for Concorde prototypes. *May*: Pre-production Concorde design announced.

1966 Manufacturer – and airline engineering liaison established. *April*: Final assembly of prototype 001 begins, Toulouse. *June*: Concorde flight simulator commissioned. *August*: Assembly of prototype 002 begins at Filton. *September*: First flight of Avro Vulcan testbed with Olympus 593 engine. *October*: Olympus 593 achieves 35,190 lb thrust on test at Bristol. *December*: Fuselage section delivered to RAE, Farnborough for fatigue testing.

1967
Design for pre-production aircraft revised to reduce drag; rear fuselage extended; new nose/visor. *February*: Concorde interior mock-up presented to airlines at Filton. *April*: Complete Olympus 593 engine first test-run in high altitude chamber, Saclay. *December 11*: 001 rolled out at Toulouse. British partner adopted 'Concorde' spelling.

1968
February: UK Government announces £125m loan for Concorde production. *August*: 001 taxi trials, Toulouse. *September*: rolled out at Toulouse. British aircraft design redefined. *December*: Olympus 593 ground-testing reaches 5,000 hours. *December 31*: First flight of Tupolev Tu-144 prototype.

1969
March 2: First flight of 001, Toulouse. *March*: Government authority given for construction of nine airframes (two ground test airframes, two prototypes, two pre-production aircraft and three production aircraft). *April 9*: First flight of 002, Filton (to Fairford). *June*: First public appearance of both prototypes, Paris air show. *October 1*: 001 achieves Mach 1. *November 8*: Airline pilots fly 001. *December*: Authority given for construction of three more production aircraft.

1970
March 25: 002 achieves Mach 1. *September 1*: 002 appears at SBAC show, Farnborough; lands at Heathrow. *November 4*: 001 achieves Mach 2. *November 12*: 002 achieves Mach 2.

1971
January: 100th supersonic flight. *March 24*: Congress stops US supersonic transport programme. *April*: Authority given for four more production aircraft. *May 25*: 001 appears at Paris air show; flies to Dakar. *June*: Total Concorde flight test time reaches 500 hours. *August*: 100th Mach 2 flight. *September 20*: First pre-production Concorde, 01 rolled out at Filton. *December 17*: First flight of 01, Filton.

1972
February 12: 01 exceeds Mach 1. *April 13*: Production aircraft 11–16 authorised. *April 22–23*: 002 appears at Hanover air show. *May 25*: BOAC announces intention to order five Concordes. *June*: 002 sales demonstration tour of Middle East and Australia. *July 24*: China signs preliminary purchase agreement for two Concordes. *July 28*: BOAC orders five Concordes, Air France orders four. *August 28*: China signs preliminary purchase agreement for a third Concorde. *September 28*: Concorde 02 rolled out at Toulouse. *October 5*: Iran Air signs preliminary purchase agreement for two Concordes plus option on a third.

1973
January 10: First flight of 02, Toulouse. *January 22–February 24*: 002 completes 'hot and high' trials at Johannesburg. *January 31*: Pan American and TWA decide not to take up their Concorde options. *June 3*: Production Tupolev Tu 144 crashes during Paris Air Show. *June 30*: 001 flight to Fort Lamy (Chad) gives 80-minute scientific observation of solar eclipse. *September 18*: 02 leaves Paris for first US visit for opening of Dallas/Fort Worth Airport. *September 26*: Breaks Washington–Paris record (3 hr 33 min) on return flight. *October 19*: 001 retired to French Air Museum at Le Bourget. *December 6*: First flight of 201, first production Concorde.

1974
February 7–19: 02 completes low-temperature trials at Fairbanks, Alaska. *February 13*: First flight of 202, second production Concorde (G-BBDG). *June 25*: Concorde static test specimen at CEAT tested to destruction. *July 19*: Initial production programme of 16 aircraft agreed. *August*: Middle East demonstration flights by 202. *September 12*: Flight testing total reaches 3,000 hours. *October 20–28*: American Pacific coast demonstration tour. *October 21*: Supersonic flight total reaches 1,000 hours.

1975
January 31: First flight of 203. *February 11*: Completion of passenger emergency evacuation certification trials. *February*: Tropical icing trials. *February 27*: First flight of 204. *February*: Certification trials at Madrid. *May 28*: Special-category C of A for 203 awarded; registration changed to F-BTSC; start of 'endurance' flying by this aircraft (completed August 2nd). *May*: Static display and flying programme at Paris air show. *June 30*: CAA special-category C of A for 204 awarded. *October 9*: Concorde receives French C of A. *October 14*: British Airways and Air France open reservations for Concorde scheduled services. *October 25*: First flight by 205. *November 5*: First flight by 206. *November 13*: Final Environmental Impact Statement published by FAA. *December 5*: Concorde receives British C of A. *December 19*: Air France receives its first Concorde (205).

1976
January 5: Concorde public hearing held by US Secretary of Transportation. *January 6*: Air France receives 203. *January 15*: British Airways receives its first Concorde (206). *January 21*: Airline service begins; London–Bahrain (British Airways, 206) and Paris–Rio via Dakar (Air France, 205). *February 4*: Concorde services to New York and Washington for 16-months trial period approved by US Secretary of Transportation. *February 13*: British Airways receives its second Concorde (204). *March 4*: 002 retired to Science Museum (based at RN Air Station, Yeovilton). *March 6*: First flight of 207. *April 8*: Air France receives 207. *April 9*: Air France service extended to Caracas via Santa Maria, Azores. *May 18*: First flight of 208. *May 20*: 02 retired to Orly Airport, Paris. *May 24*: Transatlantic services begin, from Paris and London to Washington. *July 9*: First flight of 209. *August 3*: Air France receives 209. *August 25*: First flight of 210. *September 30*: British Airways receives its third Concorde (208). *November 30*: Fairford flight test base closed. *December 6*: British Airways receives 210. *December 8*: Concorde 203 returned by Air France to Aérospatiale.

1977
February 10: First flight of 211. *March 17*: First flight of 212. *March 26*: Air France receives 211. *July 20*: British Airways receives 212. *August 20*: 01 retired to Duxford,

under care of Imperial War Museum. *October 19*: Proving flights to New York begin. *October 26*: Singapore Airlines/BA agreement on London–Singapore flights via Bahrain announced. *November 2*: H.M. The Queen and Prince Philip return from Barbados on Concorde. *November 22*: Services to New York begin, from Paris and London. *December 9*: Service from London to Singapore via Bahrain begins.

1978
Prolonged talks on Malaysian Concorde ban. *April 21*: First flight of 214. *June 26*: First flight of 213. *August 10*: BA carries its 100,000th Concorde passenger. *September 18*: Air France receives 213. *September 20*: Air France opens service Paris to Mexico City via Washington. *December 26*: First flight of 215.

1979
January 9: US type certificate awarded. *January 12*: Braniff subsonic service between Washington and Dallas/Fort Worth inaugurated. *January 24*: BA/Singapore Airlines extension Bahrain–Singapore resumed. *February 22*: British Government announces BA to write off Concorde purchase cost; Government to receive 80 per cent of operating surpluses. *April 20*: First flight of last production Concorde (216), Filton. *September 21*: British and French Governments announce unsold aircraft and support engines to be placed with British Airways and Air France. *December 16*: BA Concorde flies London–New York in 2 hr 59 min 36 sec.

1980
February 6: British Airways receives 214. *June 1*: Braniff ceases Dallas/Fort Worth service. *June 13*: British Airways receives 216. *October 23*: Air France receives 215. *November 1*: Singapore service discontinued.

1981
January 21: Five years in airline service: 50,000 hours, 15,800 flights, 700,000 passengers. *January–February*: Evidence on Concorde presented to Commons Industry and Trade Committee. *April 14*: Report on Concorde published by Commons Industry and Trade Committee expresses dissatisfaction with cost figures and urges efforts to ensure costs are shared equally with France. Government reply in July describes committee's criticisms of forecasts as 'unwarranted'. *September 11*: Anglo-French 'summit' meeting: British and French Governments commission joint studies on future of Concorde. *October 29*: British and French ministers meet in London to discuss Concorde. Three options proposed: (1) cancellation; (2) a phased rundown; (3) indefinite continuation. *December 2*: British Government review of relative costs presented to Parliament by Department of Industry. *December 9*: Department of Industry ministers and officials give evidence to Commons Industry and Trade Committee.

1982

March 31: Air France services to Caracas and Rio discontinued. *February:* British Industry and Trade Committee reaffirm dissatisfaction with cost aspects. *May 1:* Formation of Concorde Division within British Airways, responsible for profitability of Concorde operations. *May 6:* British and French ministers meet in Paris to discuss Concorde (cost reductions, officials's report, cost-sharing). *Aug:* Ian Sproat (Government Minister responsible) writes to Chairman of BA Sir John King stating that the Government will cease to fund Concorde's British manufacturers (Rolls-Royce and British Aerospace). *Oct:* Sir John King replies to the Sproat letter saying that BA will examine the possibility of Concorde funding the support costs out of revenue. *Nov:* Group set up within BA to examine support costs.

1983

Jan 1: Fastest transatlantic crossing west to east: New York to London in 2 hours 56 minutes. *April 13:* BBC television documentary about Concorde in the QED series broadcast.

1984

March 27: Concorde inaugural to Miami through Washington. Henceforward a thrice weekly service to Miami. *March 31:* After eighteen months of negotiations British Government involvement in the Concorde project becomes minimal with BA becoming responsible for funding Concorde's British manufacturers. *Sept 11:* Distance record Washington-Nice by G-BOAB 3,965 nm (4,565 statute miles). *Nov 16:* Concorde (G-BOAB) inaugural charter to Seattle from London via New York.

1985

Feb 13: First commercial service London-Sydney by Concorde under charter establishing a record time of 17 hours and 3 minutes. *March 28:* Concorde under a commercial charter establishes the record between London and Cape Town of 8 hours and 8 minutes. *April 25:* New livery unveiled by Concorde G-BOAG (214) returning into service. This aircraft had been out of service for a long period with much of its equipment having been removed for use in the other Concordes. *May 11:* Concorde special charter inaugural to Pittsburgh. *Dec 19:* Highest recorded ground speed, to date, achieved by Concorde G-BOAC in commercial service, 1,292 kt (1,488 mph).

Throughout 1985 Concorde inaugurates several routes within Europe for publicity reasons and to destinations within the Americas in conjunction with the Cunard Shipping Line.

1986

Jan 21: Concode celebrates 10 years of commercial operations. *April 5:* First Concorde charter to New Zealand, viewing Halley's Comet over the Indian Ocean. *July 11:* Prime Minister Margaret Thatcher makes her first supersonic flight on Concorde from London to Vancouver to visit EXPO 86. She is presented with a copy of the Concorde Story. *Nov 8-23:* Concorde's first round-the-world charter, special edition of The Concorde Story commissioned by John Player to mark the event.

1987

Jan: Concorde spearheads advertising for the privatisation of British Airways. *March 7:* Second round-the-world trip by Concorde, organised by Goodwood Travel. *Sept 6:* Captain Brian Walpole sets new transatlantic record – just 95 minutes between Hopedale, Newfoundland, and the Northwest Irish Coast. *Oct 5:* A BA Concorde carries the one millionth transatlantic scheduled passenger – Patrick Mannix of Reuters. *Nov 22:* Concorde celebrates tenth anniversary of operations into John F. Kennedy International, New York, Richard Noble, landspeed record holder, sets new record by crossing the Atlantic three times in one day – on Concorde. *Dec 12:* Concorde commences new scheduled service, once weekly to Barbados for the winter season.

1988

Feb 7: Concorde G-BOAA makes record New York to Heathrow flight: 2 hr 55 min 15 sec. *April:* G-BOAA, first Concorde to undergo 12,000 flying hours check. Structure pronounced sound for service well into 21st century. *June 15:* Inaugural Concorde twice weekly to Dallas, Texas, for summer period till August. *June:* Captain Walpole awarded OBE in Queen's Birthday honours. *Dec:* Concorde resumes Barbados service for winter season. Captain Walpole retires from BA.

1989

Feb: Noel Edmonds features Captain John Hutchinson on BBC programme about Concorde, aviation and travel. *March 2:* Aerospatiale host party to celebrate 20th anniversary of Concorde's first flight at Toulouse in 1969. *March:* HM Queen flies to Barbados on Concorde. *April 1:* Concorde leaves Heathrow on supersonic circumnavigation charter – to cover 38,343 miles. *April:* Concorde loses part of rudder between Auckland and Sydney, circumnavigation continues safely after repair. *Nov 19:* Channel 4 TV 'Faster than a Speeding Bullet' by Captain Christopher Orlebar features Concorde in the History and future of supersonic flight.

1990

Jan 21: Concorde celebrates 14th anniversary of commercial service. *Jan:* The largest charterer of Concorde, Goodwood Travel, announce that they have now carried 37,153 passengers on Concorde.

March 2: Concorde 21 years old today, Concorde 001 first flight at Toulouse in 1969. *April 6:* Prince Michael of Kent presents awards to Concorde engineers. *April 14:* Capt Norman Britton takes New York to London record 2hr 54min 30sec. *May 5:* BAe & Aerospatiale unveil plans for Concorde successor; BA will take 'more than usual interest'. *June 1:* Concorde Honolulu to Hong Kong in 6hr 30min (subsonic time 13hr 10min). *June 6:* Celebration of 50th anniversary of Battle of Britain, Capt Jock Lowe flies Concorde in formation with Spitfire over the White Cliff's of Dover. *Aug 10:* Concorde assists at Gatwick Airport's diamond jubilee, pictured with a de Havilland Dragon Rapide. *Sept 7:* Concorde model installed at Heathrow's main entrance roundabout. *Sept 14:* Concorde appears at Farnborough airshow. *Nov 30:* Concorde twice weekly winter services to Barbados recommence.

1991

Jan 11: Announcement that Concorde Washington to Miami services will cease as from March 31. *Jan:* Second rudder on Concorde delaminates. *April 4:* Capt Hutchinson – president of Skyfliers Club – flies competition winners to Washington to celebrate Concorde's 15th anniversary of commercial flights. *May 5:* Capt W D (Jock) Lowe becomes director of flight crew BA. *May 14:* HM Queen & HRH Prince Philip in Concorde to Washington to start official tour of USA, Capt Lowe i/c. *June 7:* New computerised Concorde flight planning system introduced. *June 28:* Concorde appears on hat at Ascot (as a milliners miniature). *July 12:* Concorde 101 – the fastest and highest ever Concorde (M2.23 and 12+ miles on test) at Duxford repainted. *July 12:* Concorde summer services (11) to Toronto announced. *July 19:* Gen Sir Peter de la Billiere awards 100 prize draw award LHR-JFK tickets to Gulf War veterans. *July 26:* Two Concorde flights to Jeddah. *Aug 23:* G-BOAA receives four coats of paint. *Aug 30:* Marriage vicar stewards his newly weds on Concorde – 'Wing & a prayer'. *Sep 20:* Concorde 'the most valuable BA asset' is protected with improved security fences at LHR. *Oct 4:* Concorde weekly winter service to Barbados will be via Lisbon for the 91/92 season. *Oct 18:* IMF bankers to Bangkok on Concorde. *Nov 1:* Capt Lowe hosts Jackie Mann – former Beirut hostage – on Concorde. *Dec 12:* Capt Hutchinson breaks record, Acapulco to Honolulu via Las Vegas and Capt Musson, Bali to Colombo via Mombasa; Lord King awards FAI certificates.

1992

Jan 22: Mary Goldring, former fierce critic, looks forward to a Concorde successor in her TV programme 'Goldring's Audit'. *Feb 21:* Capt Hutchinson nearing retirement & noted for TV appearances on Concorde, makes BBC World Service programme: 'A personal view'. *March:* Concorde to visit Nigeria & South Africa. *March 27:* Neil Kinnock electioneering for Labour party visits BA Concorde. *April 9:* Tories win general election. *July 17:* Capts Horton, Hutchinson & Musset – Concorde speed record holders – to Buckingham Palace garden party. *July:* Former BOAC chairman Sir Basil Smallpiece dies. *Sept 9:* Concorde G-BOAF to have new set of insulation blankets. *Nov 11:* Concorde pulled 440 yds by RAF team for Children in Need Charity. *Dec 18:* Concorde to Barbados again for winter with one extension to Mexico at end of March '93.

1993

Jan 29: Lord King, pictured with Concorde model tucked under arm, is honoured for Outstanding Contribution to International Aviation during Chairmanship of BA; he is to become President of BA for life. *March 26:* Senior First Officer Barbara Harmer of BA becomes first lady pilot of Concorde. *May 21:* Concorde G-BOAF to become first of seven to have £1m internal and external refurbishment. *July 2:* Capt Rowland becomes Concorde business manager. *July 30:* Rush of cabin crew to serve on Concorde. *Aug 27:* Concorde human to to raise money for BA's Charity 'Dreamflight'. *Sept 12:* Capt Orlebar, former Concorde First Officer, consultant for 'Your Flight', Channel 4 documentary on Air Traffic Control. *Oct 10:* Special flight Concorde to Jeddah. *Nov 12:* Concorde with Capt Morris at Athens celebrating 60th anniversary of Greek association, first flight took 50 h, cf Concorde's 2h 27m. *Nov 19:* G-BOAA receives new £1M upper rudder, solution to previous rudder problem. *Dec 3:* Fastest show on earth – Bee Gees flight around Bay of Biscay organised by Concorde Flight Engineer Bill Brown – celebrations raising £48,000 for Children in Need.

1994

Jan 7: Concorde BA001 LHR to JFK first with the new Cabin Crew uniform. *Feb 4:* Student from Southampton awarded Sword of Honour on Concorde's flight deck. *March 2:* 25th anniversary of Concorde 001's first flight from Toulouse is celebrated. *April 7:* Aerospatiale, British Aerospace and Deutsche Aerospace announce agreement on supersonic research for son of Concorde.

British Airways (BA) Concorde destinations from London (Heathrow) Airport

1994 Scheduled Services
Barbados (often via Lisbon westbound, non stop eastbound) *once weekly or more during winter season.*
New York *twice daily for most of the year.*
Toronto *various schedules over summer months.*
Washington *thrice weekly.*

Past scheduled services:
Bahrain
Dallas Fort Worth (via Washington with BA, then Braniff)
Miami (via Washington)
Singapore (via Bahrain)

Diversions:
Atlantic City
Bangor
Boston
Gander
Gatwick
Halifax
Lajes
Montreal
Newark
Shannon
Windsor Locks

Charter Destinations:
Africa:
Abidjan
Aswan
Cairo
Capetown
Dakar
Harare
Johannesburg
Kilimanjaro
Luxor
Marrakesh
Mombasa
Nairobi
Robertsville (Monrovia)

The Americas:
Abbotsford
Acapulco
Antigua
Aruba
Ashville
Atlanta
Atlantic City
Austin (Texas)
Baltimore
Bangor
Barbados
Bermuda
Boston
Buffalo
Calgary
Charleston
Cincinatti
Cleveland
Colorado Springs
Columbus
Dayton
Detroit
Fort Lauderdale
Fort Myers
Goose Bay
Grand Cayman
Harrisburg
Honolulu
Houston Ellington
Indianapolis
Jacksonville
Kingston
Las Vegas
Lexington
Lima
Mexico City
Miami
Montego Bay
Montreal
Nashville
Nassau
New Orleans
New York
Oakland
Oklahoma City
Omaha
Ontario (USA)
Orlando
Oshkosh
Ottawa
Philadelphia
Phoenix
Pittsburg
Portland
Port of Spain
Providence
Puerto Rico
Raleigh
Richmond
Rio de Janeiro
Rochester
Rockford
St Lucia
Santa Maria
Schenectady
Seattle
Springfield
Syracuse
Tahiti
Tampa
Tampa Macdill
Toronto
Trinidad
Vancouver
Waco
Washington
Washington Andrews
Windsor Locks
Windsor Ontario

Australasia:
Auckland
Brisbane
Christchurch
Fiji
Learmonth
Perth
Sydney

Europe and Middle East:
Amman
Amsterdam
Ancona
Aqaba
Bahrain
Barcelona
Basle
Berlin
Billund
Bologna
Bordeaux
Bratislava
Brussels
Budapest
Cologne
Copenhagen
Dhahran
Faro
Graz
Hanover
Helsinki
Istanbul
Jeddah
Keflavik
Kuwait
Larnaca
Leipzig
Leningrad
Linz
Lisbon
Luxembourg
Madrid
Malaga
Milan
Moscow
Munich
Munster
Nice
Oporto
Oslo
Palma
Paris
Pescara
Prague
Riyadh
Rome
Rovaniemi
Salzburg
Seville
Stavanger
Stockholm
Strasbourg
Tel Aviv
Toulouse
Tours
Turin

Vasteras
Venice
Vienna
Warsaw

Far East:
Bali
Bangkok
Beijing
Bombay
Colombo
Delhi
Djakarta
Guam
Hong Kong
Kula Lumpur
Singapore
Tashkent

United Kingdom:
Belfast
Birmingham
Brize Norton
Cardiff
Coltishall
East Midlands
Edinburgh
Exeter
Fairford
Farnborough
Filton
Finningley
Gatwick
Glasgow
Humberside
Leeds
Leuchars
Liverpool
Luton
Macrihanish
Manchester
Manston
Mildenhall
Newcastle
Prestwick
St Mawgan
Stansted
Teeside
Yeovilton

Air France Concorde destinations from Charles de Gaulle Airport (Paris)

1994 Scheduled Service New York *once daily*

Past Scheduled Services: Caracas (via Santa Maria), Mexico (via Washington), Rio de Janeiro (via Dakar), Washington

Note: Air France also handles Concorde charters, but these have not been listed here

---

Bibliography

An Introduction to the Slender, Delta Transport, BAC/ Aerospatiale, 1975

British Airways and Concorde Finances, Report of the Review Group, Department of Trade and Industry, February 1984.

David Beaty, *The Water Jump*, Secker & Warburg, 1976.

Charles Burnet, *Three Centuries to Concorde*, MEP, 1979.

Dr. P. H. Calder and P. C. Gupta, Future SST Engines, SAE, 1975.

Brian Calvert, Flying Concorde, Airlife, 1981.

Concorde, Second Report from the Industry and Trade Committee, Session 1980-81.

Flight International – various articles.

P.C. Gupta, Rolls-Royce Ltd., Aero Div., Bristol, *Advanced Olympus for Next Generation Supersonic Transport Aircraft*, SAE, 1981.

History of Aviation, New English Library, 1972.

Sir Stanley Hooker, *Not Much of an Engineer*, Airlife, 1984.

Jane's All the World's aircraft – various editions.

Geoffrey Knight, *Concorde, The Inside Story*, Weidenfeld & Nicholson, 1976.

Sir Frank Whittle, *Jet, the Story of a Pioneer*, (Frederick Muller, 1953).

C. S. Leyman BAe, Bristol, *After Concorde What Next?*, (Presentation at A.I.A.A. annual meeting, Washington, 1985).

J. E. Morpurgo, *Barnes Wallace*, Longman, 1972.

Kenneth Owen, Concorde, *New Shape in the Sky*, Jane's, 1982).

Richard H. Peterson and Cornelius Driver, *Advanced Supersonic Transport Status*, (Presentation at A.I.A.A. annual meeting, Washington April, 1985).

Arthur Reed, *Britain's Aircraft Industry, What went Right? What went Wrong?*, Dent 1973.

Darrol Sinton, *The Anatomy of the Aeroplane*, Granada, 1966 (reprinted 1980).

Sir Basil Smallpiece, *Of Comets and Queens*, Airlife, 1981.

Index

Illustration acknowledgements

Photographs and diagrams were kindly
supplied by the following: *Aeroplane*;
Aerospace Publishing Ltd; Peter A. Bisset; The
Boeing Company; Alan Bond; Braniff
International; British Aerospace; British Tourist
Authority; Avions Marcel Dassault; *Flight*
International; Image in Industry; International Air
Radio Ltd; Jack Leffler/Sky Eye Aerial
Photographers; Adrian Meredith Photography;
Metro Dade County; M. L. Nathan; National
Aeronautics and Space Administration;
Christopher Orlebar; Nigel Paige; Christine
Quick Photography Ltd; RAF Mu[...]
Rolls-Royce; Jeppesen Sanderson[...]
Southampton University; Tony S[...]
Syndication International; Micha[...]
Mark Wagner.

Index

Illustration acknowledgements

Photographs and diagrams were kindly supplied by the following: *Aeroplane*; Aerospace Publishing Ltd; Peter A. Bisset; The Boeing Company; Alan Bond; Braniff International; British Aerospace; British Tourist Authority; Avions Marcel Dassault; *Flight International*; Image in Industry; International Air Radio Ltd; Jack Leffler/Sky Eye Aerial Photographers; Adrian Meredith Photography; Metro Dade County; M. L. Nathan; National Aeronautics and Space Administration; Christopher Orlebar; Nigel Paige; Christine Quick Photography Ltd; RAF Museum; Rolls-Royce; Jeppesen Sanderson Inc; Southampton University; Tony Stone Associates; Syndication International; Michael Taylor; Mark Wagner.